THE BOND OF PEACE

THE SEVEN ONES FROM EPHESIANS 4

BEREAN STUDY SERIES

The Bond of Peace: The Seven Ones in Ephesians 4

Published by Heritage Christian University

Copyright © 2026 by Heritage Christian University Press

Manufactured in the United States of America

Cataloging-in-Publication Data

The Bond of Peace: The Seven Ones in Ephesians 4/

Berean Study Series

p. cm.

Includes scripture index.

ISBN 979-8-89733-019-5 (pbk.) 979-8-89733-020-1 (ebook)

1. Bible. Ephesians 4—Study and teaching. 2. Christian life—Study and teaching I. Title. II. Series.

227.5007—dc20

Library of Congress Control Number: 2026933930

Cover design by Brad McKinnon.

For information:

Heritage Christian University Press

3625 Helton Drive, PO Box HCU, Florence, AL 35630

www.hcu.edu

Contents

INTRODUCTION
ED GALLAGHER

The New Testament is about the church. Now, don't get me wrong: it's about some other things, too. If you said that the New Testament is about Christ, I wouldn't argue with you. The Apostle Paul once said, "I determined not to know anything among you, save Jesus Christ, and him crucified" (1 Corinthians 2:2). And if you said that God is the main theme of the New Testament, I could defend the point. Or maybe you think it would be best to identify the main topic of the New Testament as not God or Christ exactly but something about them—perhaps the Atonement or the grace of God. All of this makes sense to me. But I still say the New Testament is about the church.

Christ died to form the church. "And I, if I be lifted up from the earth, will draw all men unto me" (John 12:32). So said our Lord, and the Evangelist offers this interpretation: "This he said, signifying what death he should die" (12:33). The death of Jesus drew people to him, and these people are the church, the community who enjoys the blessings of Atonement, upon whom God pours out his grace. Saying that the New Testament is about Christ's crucifixion or about God's grace does not mean that it's not about the church; it's a matter of emphasis. But certainly the New Testament emphasizes the church. Think about this: every single one of the writings of the New Testament were written for the church, the people of God, to edify Christians in their faith. Many of the New Testament writings were originally directed to specific churches (mostly Paul's letters, also Revelation). Moreover, the message of Jesus, in summary, was this: "The time is fulfilled, and the kingdom of God is at hand: repent ye, and believe the gospel" (Mark 1:15). Who are those people who have repented and believed the gospel? What is the group of people called over whom Christ reigns as king, who are, therefore, a part of the kingdom of God? The New Testament applies to these people the Greek term *ekklesia*, often translated "church." Jesus himself—at least in Greek translation (assuming Jesus actually taught in Aramaic)—applied this very term to the community of his followers (Matthew 16:18, 18:17). I say it again: the New Testament is about the church.

And what does the New Testament say to the church? Yes, it has much to say about the grace of God, and the crucifixion and resurrection of Jesus, and the good news that Christ now sits at the right hand of God, interceding on behalf of his people. "All power is given unto me in heaven and in earth," exclaims Jesus following his Passion (Matthew 28:18). The church needs to know all of this; these are things the church should believe, teachings that should shape Christian identity. But what is it that the church should do? What are the responsibilities of the church?

Here, again, there could be several answers. Some people will want to emphasize evangelism, perhaps in reliance on the Great Commission (Matthew 28:19).

Others will nominate worship as a primary task of God's people, citing it as our destiny in the hereafter, as the book of Revelation suggests (Revelation 4–5). Some will want to talk about the church as the "hands and feet" of Jesus, in reliance on Paul's image of the church as the body of Christ (especially in 1 Corinthians 12), and so the church should do good in the world (cf. Matthew 25:31–46) as Jesus did (Acts 10:38). Yes, yes yes! But, in the New Testament, even greater stress—greater than any of these aforementioned points—is laid on another aspect of church responsibility.

Unity.

What is the church supposed to do? It's supposed to be united. Christians are supposed to love one another. I think it would be fair to say that this is the main theme of all of Paul's letters. I mean, he definitely wants to talk about Christ crucified, because the crucifixion is important to us individually, and we rejoice that God was willing to send his son for that purpose, because he loved us, and we marvel that Jesus was willing to endure that suffering on our behalf. And yet, why did Paul want to emphasize Christ crucified to the Corinthians? It's because the Corinthian church was divided into different factions (1 Corinthians 1:11), and Paul thought that people who acclaim as Lord one who suffered death for others could not possibly get into arguments with each other about who's faction is better or who best represents Jesus, as the Twelve had earlier (Luke 22:24). If you're willing to exalt yourself over your brother, then you clearly haven't reflected enough on the crucifixion of Jesus. That's why Paul determined to know nothing but Christ crucified. It was for the purpose of church unity.

Or think about that famous Christ Hymn passage in Philippians 2, the one that shows Jesus emptying himself as he dispensed with his divine prerogatives and submitted to a slave's death (Phil 2:6–11). Why did Paul bring up this account of Jesus? Why mention it here to the Philippians? Paul tells us: he wants the Philippian Christians to "let this mind be in you, which was also in Christ Jesus." He wants the Philippian church to imitate Jesus in self-emptying. Why? Church unity. "If there be therefore any consolation in Christ, if any comfort of love, if any fellowship of the Spirit, if any bowels and mercies, Fulfil ye my joy, that ye be likeminded, having the same love, being of one accord, of one mind" (Philippians 2:1–2). The Philippian church, like the church in Corinth, was experiencing some strife, associated with two leading women (4:2), and it was of the utmost importance that the situation not split the church. It was imperative that the body of Christ remain one.

Paul addresses the same subject in Ephesians. The point of the church is to represent Christ in the world, which means that the church needs to grow into the image of Christ. Lord knows—and Paul knows—that this will take growth, because we ain't there yet. But he lays out the goal this way.

> But speaking the truth in love, [we] may grow up into him in all things, which is the head, even Christ: From whom the whole body fitly joined together and compacted by that which every joint supplieth, according to the effectual working in the measure of every part, maketh increase of the body unto the edifying of itself in love. (Ephesians 4:15–16)

We, the church, are the body of Christ, and we are growing into our role as the body of Christ. This image of the church as Christ's body is itself an illustration of the unity that needs to pertain within the church, as Paul expounds in 1 Corinthians 12, leading to the programmatic declaration, "Now ye are the body of Christ, and members in particular" (1 Corinthians 12:27). What Paul means in 1 Corinthians is that our role as the body of Christ has very definite implications about how we treat one another, how we love one another, how we rejoice with those who rejoice and weep with those who weep. Again, church unity.

And he means the same thing in Ephesians 4 by the image of God's people as the body of Christ. It is for the purpose of church unity that God distributed different gifts to different people (Ephesians 4:7–12), "Till we all come in the unity of the faith, and of the knowledge of the Son of God, unto a perfect man, unto the measure of the stature of the fulness of Christ (4:13). Paul starts this passage by highlighting the humility that Christians should display toward one another, so that they may "keep the unity of the Spirit in the bond of peace" (4:3). In Ephesians 4, Paul is on his constant theme, the topic he never leaves, the unity of the church.

The hope for the world is a church united, loving one another, representing Christ.

The greatest threat to the world is a divided church.

Paul is on his constant theme in Ephesians 4, but that's not to say that he doesn't have new ways of addressing the familiar topic. In this passage, the apostle mentions seven aspects of Christian faith and practice that bind believers together (Ephesians 4:4–6).

- There is one body.
- There is one Spirit.
- There is one hope.
- There is one faith.
- There is one Lord.

- There is one baptism.
- There is one God.

In Ephesians, Paul lists these seven Ones so quickly that he spends no time exploring them. Perhaps he had preached on these topics many times before in the hearing of the recipients of this letter. But those expositions are not preserved for us. And yet these seven Ones that are supposed to ground the church's unity deserve our thoughtful attention.

We try to supply some thoughtful attention to these topics in the chapters that follow. Let me explain the structure of the book, which is similar to previous installments of the Berean Study Series but with a little tweak. We asked each author to write a pair of chapters on the assigned topic, the first chapter addressing the topic in general (whether body or Spirit or hope, etc.) and the second chapter addressing how "oneness" relates to the subject. Why does Paul say that there is "one" body? Or "one" Spirit? What is he denying? What is he affirming? How does—or ought— the "oneness" of the body or the Spirit or the faith (etc.) contribute to Christian unity? We hope this approach to the seven Ones of Ephesians 4 proves stimulating and helpful to you in your personal Bible study and for the people to whom you minister.

And we hope that this series of studies contributes to the building up of the body of Christ so that it may keep the unity of the Spirit in the bond of peace.

THE CHRISTIAN BODY
JEREMY BARRIER

SUMMARY

While Ephesians is not the only letter within the Pauline corpus of writings to emphasize the 'Body of Christ', it is, nonetheless, arguably, the most succinct and well-stated letter that addresses unity in the body. Unity within the body of Christ is necessary 1) for the living spirit of God to dwell within and consequently, 2) for the body of Christ to then carry out the work of God on earth.

FOCUS PASSAGES

And [God the Father] hath put all things under [Jesus'] feet, and gave him to be the head over all things to the church, which is his body, the fulness of him that filleth all in all.

Therefore, the prisoner of the Lord, beseech you that ye walk worthy of the vocation wherewith ye are called, with all lowliness and meekness, with longsuffering, forbearing one another in love; endeavouring to keep the unity of the Spirit in the bond of peace. There is one body, and one Spirit, even as ye are called in one hope of your calling; one Lord, one faith, one baptism, one God and Father of all, who is above all, and through all, and in you all.

...till we all come in the unity of the faith, and of the knowledge of the Son of God, unto a perfect man, unto the measure of the stature of the fulness of Christ. That we henceforth be no more children, tossed to and fro, and carried about with every wind of doctrine, by the sleight of men, and cunning craftiness, whereby they lie in wait to deceive; but speaking the truth in love, may grow up into him in all things, which is the head, even Christ: from whom the whole body fitly joined together and compacted by that which every joint supplieth, according to the effectual working in the measure of every part, maketh increase of the body unto the edifying of itself in love.

Ephesians 1:22–23; 4:1–6, 13–16 (KJV)

ONE MAIN THING

The entire body (i.e., the church)—from the thorax to the pelvis, along with the arms, legs, hands, and feet—is connected to a head, and it is clearly Jesus Christ. Each breath he takes brings the spirit of God into His lungs, and he is alive, healthy, and mature. The body of Christ, a singular person, can now move forward into the world to do good unto all of humanity.

INTRODUCTION

One of the greatest joys of my life has been holding my children when they were infants. The calm, peace, and serenity that is felt while holding a soft, small, glowing child is indescribable. Although it has been two decades now, I can remember holding my daughter while she slept in my arms. I would find a chair to sit in and hold her comfortably, while she slept. Then I could just sit and observe. Each steady and calm expansion of the chest, breathing in. Then, a slow movement of regress, breathing out. Maybe a gentle movement of the lips with a slight sucking sound. A slight movement of the arm. Then breathing in again. And out again. It was beautiful. The realization that this was life. Each breath was life. Each sound was the sound of a process of maturation that was taking place at a rate that was so slight, slow, and subtle that it couldn't be detected with the eye, but it was clearly felt in my heart. The emotions would overflow as the small being looked to me as a sun emerging from the hills beyond in the morning, and an exorbitant, overflowing light was taking over the world and filling my heart at the same time. I am talking about the miracle of life. The radiance. The joy. The perfection that comes about through the breath of life filling the child's lungs one gasp at a time.

To state my thoughts more directly, I am enamored, perplexed, and overjoyed by the beauty of a new life in a small body that lives and functions. God is *moving in* that child with each breath and bringing it up to a point of maturity. This is a point of completion, when finally, 21 years later, a parent 'unleashes' their child into the world, and when they successfully move into their adult life, they have arrived. They are a complete, mature young adult, who has been designed by God to *honor the Creator in their life* and *do God unto all of God's creation, especially humanity.*

GOING DEEPER

If you cannot discern the movements within my heart, allow me to explain. I am trying to express the joy I felt as a parent seeing, truly seeing, the beauty of life through the human body. The image of the human body is one of the dominant themes that is clearly in the mind of God when he inspired the apostle Paul to put 'pen to paper' and write the letter to the Ephesians. We know for a fact, as explicitly stated by Paul in 1 Corinthians 12 (not to mention a host of other places in 1 Corinthians), that the 'church' being the 'body of Christ' is an essential and important theme. If the church will 'work together' and submit itself under Christ, then we begin to function as a body, working in unison, to accomplish a specific goal; whether this be walking, running, sitting, eating, etc. However, if one looks closely in Ephesians, it becomes clear that the concept of a human body is clearly serving as a template or backdrop for the entire letter! Notice the passages listed above (and also the passages listed in the next lesson, too!), and one begins to see that the idea of the body is prevalent from the first chapter to the last.

> [God the Father] hath put all things *under* [Jesus's] *feet*, and gave him to be *the head* over all things to the church, *which is his body*, the fulness of him that filleth all in all." "unto a *perfect man*, unto the measure of the *stature of the fulness of Christ* ... may grow up into him in all things, which is *the head*, even Christ: from *whom the whole body*

fitly joined together and compacted by that which every joint supplieth ....

It becomes apparent that if Christ is the head of the body, and we are the body of Christ, then there can be nothing other than one body, or the system will not work correctly. The metaphor is clear and seems to make sense if one is aware of the imagery in mind. Further, what is most impressive about this imagery is that one can take it one step further. The imagery that is essential to understand here doesn't come out of thin air, but is rather the essential 'Biblical' metaphor of creation drawn from Genesis 1–2. To be more specific, one reads in Genesis chapter two of the beautiful creation of Adam and Eve. At the moment when all has been done, the 'mud' has been molded, the arms have been shaped, the eyes have been given their final hue of color, God *breathes life* into Adam, and he lives! It is the divine breath of God! This is the very breath that enters into God's church today as the imagery of creation is clearly on the 'tip of the tongue' and is finally uttered through the thoughts of Ephesians 3:16–17, "... he may grant that you may be strengthened in your inner being with power through his *Spirit*, and that Christ may dwell in your hearts through faith, as you are being rooted and grounded in love." This is the establishment of Adam, who was 'rooted and grounded' in love, as God made him, along with Eve, to be 'perfect' vessels to carry the good of God into the world (see 2 Timothy 3:10–17; Genesis 2:7; Genesis 1:27–31).

APPLICATION

The point of all of this is for us to understand that God's intentions for Jesus Christ and us was to be one body!

Christ is the head, and we as the Church are *designed to function together as one body maturing to perfection, so that God's presence can be known here on earth.* God wants to connect with us, corporately and in community. Humans are truly gregarious creatures, and we are *meant to function in community.* God doesn't seek the 'personal' self-interested transformation of an individual, but wants the community to function. God wants to work in us and through us as a body.

CONCLUSION

As I began my thoughts in the introduction, I was thinking about my daughter in her infancy. Now, here I am, two and a half decades after the birth of our first child, and I am seeing both of my children enter into the world as complete humans. *Young* adults, no doubt, with so much yet to learn (!), but fully capable and functional to *learn what is necessary to grow,* and at the same time to begin functioning and being a part of the human race. They are making choices about who they are, what they want to be, what they will stand for, who they will marry, and so forth. All of the processes of being a fully functioning human being in the world. When they reach this point, it is also as beautiful as those first still, quiet moments when they slept in my arms, and I witnessed each individual breath, one at a time. The church can grow into the body of Christ. It takes time, commitment, and a humility to prefer God's will over ours. In time, the body will mature, and the church can take its place in the world and do the work of God.

DISCUSSION

1. Read some of the specific passages mentioned above that draw from the metaphor of the human body. What parts of the body are mentioned?
2. What is the point of comparing the church to a human body?
3. How are Christians today able to function 'as one' when we choose to work with the body of Christ?
4. Why do you think Christ is mentioned to be the 'head' in this figure of speech? What role does a head have to a body? How do they function together?

Only One Body?

Jeremy Barrier

Summary

While Ephesians is not the only letter within the Pauline corpus of writings to emphasize the 'Body of Christ', it is, nonetheless, arguably, the most succinct and well-stated letter that addresses unity in the body. Unity within the body of Christ is necessary 1) for the living spirit of God to dwell within and consequently 2) for the body of Christ to then carry out the work of God on earth.

Focus passage

> And [God the Father] hath put all things under [Jesus'] feet, and gave him to be the head over all things to the church, which is his body, the fulness of him that filleth all in all.
>
> Therefore, the prisoner of the Lord, beseech you that ye walk worthy of the vocation wherewith ye are called, with all lowliness and meekness, with longsuffering,

forbearing one another in love; endeavouring to keep the unity of the Spirit in the bond of peace. There is one body, and one Spirit, even as ye are called in one hope of your calling; one Lord, one faith, one baptism, one God and Father of all, who is above all, and through all, and in you all.

Finally, my brethren, be strong in the Lord, and in the power of his might. Put on the whole armour of God, that ye may be able to stand against the wiles of the devil. For we wrestle not against flesh and blood, but against principalities, against powers, against the rulers of the darkness of this world, against spiritual wickedness in high places. Wherefore take unto you the whole armour of God, that ye may be able to withstand in the evil day, and having done all, to stand. Stand therefore, having your loins girt about with truth, and having on the breastplate of righteousness; and your feet shod with the preparation of the gospel of peace; above all, taking the shield of faith, wherewith ye shall be able to quench all the fiery darts of the wicked. And take the helmet of salvation, and the sword of the Spirit, which is the word of God.

Ephesians 1:22–23; 4:1–6; 6:10–17 (KJV)

One Main Thing (Again)

The entire body (i.e., the church)—from the thorax to the pelvis, along with the arms, legs, hands, and feet—is connected to a head, and it is clearly Jesus Christ. Each breath he takes brings the spirit of God into His lungs, and he is alive, healthy, and mature. The body of Christ, a singular person, can now move forward into the world to do good unto all of humanity.

Introduction

Thomas was observing the folds of the leather that ran parallel to his leg. The color was an ash gray, in contrast to the felt fabric that was a darker charcoal gray just to the right of the ash gray leather. He was watching it intently. So intently that he noticed the slightest stains of darkness that marred the carpeted portion. The uneven patchwork of dark colors was no doubt the coffee stains from two weeks ago, when mom had attempted to intervene in the backseat of the car—from the driver's seat no less—to intervene in a conflict over the very line that Thomas was observing now. We had been sitting at the red light for at least 30 seconds when Carolyn, my sister, had finally found the courage to move her left-hand pinky about a quarter of an inch *over the line*, and I called her out on it! Mom turned quickly, somewhat shocked by my screaming, and in the process managed to move Carolyn's hand *back to her side* of the car, while also spilling the coffee in her Yeti at the same time. If the coffee stains weren't a sign enough that Carolyn should stay on her side, and I on mine, then I don't know what would work! All I knew was that her pinky finger was hovering, again, incredibly close to the line, and I was about to call her out. This was simply not right. It wasn't fair. This was *my side of the backseat of the car*, and that was her side. She should stay on her side!

I realize that this scenario above may appear to trivialize the sense of 'right' and 'wrong' that most humans feel, but I assure you, this feeling and sense often do not diminish in many of us. Whether we are nine years old (as is my young 'Thomas' above) or 69 years old, we feel a sense of justice. All one needs to do is look at the daily headlines in the papers. Here in the year 2026, not a day goes by that I don't see headlines filled with emotion that are addressing 'lines' of demarcation between Russia, Ukraine, and Nato countries; Lebanon, Israel, Syria, and Gaza, or even the United States of America from Mexico. Trivializing the human sense of justice will get us nowhere. Rather, recognizing that there is an innate gift of God may be the better choice, and determining how to address these injustices will be the groundwork for resolution.

Going one step further, I mention all of this as a prelude to the topic of this chapter: Unity and "Oneness" in the body of Christ. Is there only one body? When we take into consideration the thoughts that I mentioned above about boundary disputes between children and adults, we begin to get a sense of how complicated is the matter of unifying the church, let alone humanity. Let's go a little deeper into this issue, while we also reflect on Ephesians 4:4–6.

GOING DEEPER

In Ephesians 4:4–6, we have the seven glorious "ones" which are held before us as a beacon of aspiration. They are both an ideal, yet also a reality that *must* be attained in order for Christ to work effectively in this world. As I stated in the previous chapter, the metaphor of the human body runs throughout Ephesians, and in the passages of Scripture above, I highlight one or two additional passages to exemplify this. In chapter six of Ephesians, God's spirit gives us a deep and beautiful insight that not only builds on the creation of Adam (see the previous chapter), but even extends these ideas! Not only has God formed and made humanity with Christ as the head—with all of us, as the Church, being joined together through ligaments and sinews to Christ as the body—, but once the body is formed, then God 'fits' it out with weapons! By the time we arrive at chapter six, we realize that the metaphor was not simply of the creation of a human, but the human that has been formed, and is now ready to do good, is specifically being equipped to go into battle! The battle of good versus evil. This is the battle of justice versus injustice. This is the battle where the "Evil One" (Ephesians 6:16) is apocalyptically opposing the armies of God. Thus, you put on your armor, which includes a belt, breastplate, shoes, a shield, a helmet, and a sword. All of this will assist the body of Christ as they oppose the "cosmic powers of this present darkness, against the spiritual forces of evil in the heavenly places" (6:12). The body must be unified to fight the forces of evil.

Yet, this is where that sense of 'right' and 'wrong' not only fuels us for good, but sometimes foils us as well. Is the body one? When the words of Ephesians were written that the body of Christ should be one, and only one, the realities of the present, divergent Christendom were over a millennium away. Yet as time has moved forward, Christians have divided themselves based on a sense of 'right' and 'wrong' pertaining to our teachings and systems of belief. When we look at nominal Christendom today, the variation is astounding. A total of 2.4 billion people profess Jesus as Lord and Son of the Father. Further, there are approximately 1.4 billion Catholics, 250 million Orthodox Christians, and 750 million Protestants. As a branch, often categorized within Protestantism, Churches of Christ represent some 3–4 million people globally, a tiny sliver in the midst of the Christian population. Further, statistics suggest that there are somewhere between 9,000 and 50,000 denominations within Protestantism!

This is the moment where our sense of 'right' and 'wrong' becomes difficult for us. We know that Christ called for there to be one body, yet Christianity is so fragmented! What can be done? I would suggest that we learn to differentiate between the real and the ideal. I have lived long enough to realize that there are great discrepancies between what a 'local church' ought to be and what it is. The teachings of Scripture inspire us to live to be a better version of ourselves than we are on most days. I wish that churches didn't have internal conflict, marriages being destroyed, gossip tearing communities apart, and so forth. However, these things do happen and exist within the church. This is why the grace of God (and grace that comes from us toward one another) is so critical for the functioning of the body. *We aspire to be the body of Christ discussed in Ephesians*, and I am sure that those original recipients of the letter were inspired as well! It calls us to a higher standard! In the meantime, I think we can continue our 'restoration plea' for people to be one body, Christians only, reject creeds and sectarianism, and realize that we are attempting to live out an ideal, an essential and important ideal.

APPLICATION

When I look at the teaching that there is "One Body" in Ephesians, I am moved and impressed deep within my soul. This is a powerful teaching found not only here, but in numerous places of Scripture (1 Corinthians 3:16; John 17; etc.). We must aspire to be better and more than we typically are able to accomplish in our lives. We should call and encourage the local church to work as 'one body', while also appealing for the many churches of Christ in our communities to work as one. Further, there is still a need to call and encourage the world of nominal Christendom to also take this teaching seriously, while we strive to fight the forces of evil, rather than fight amongst ourselves.

CONCLUSION

Just this morning, in December 2025, I watched as 'peace plans' were presented and discussed for how to resolve conflict between Ukraine and Russia. One of the tenets that is being discussed is a redrawing of the borders between these two nations, where land presently claimed by Ukraine will be given to Russia. The president of Ukraine finds this deeply unsettling. It is bothering his sense of 'right' and 'wrong,' no doubt. Similarly, Thomas was bothered about his sister placing her hand on his side of the car. Further, I look at Scripture and see that the 'body of Christ' should be one and united to Christ, yet the world I live within looks so much more complicated than what is addressed in Ephesians. How am I to deal with the call for unity? How am I to deal with a teaching that *insists upon* unity in the body of Christ? I do this in two ways. First, I understand the metaphor. A body must completely be working in unison and in good health if it wants to be a force for good. Yet not only a force for good, but a body that will actively oppose the forces of evil! By understanding this metaphor, I can more fully understand what the Ephesian writer was proposing that we see and understand about the BODY OF CHRIST. Second, I also realize that while I cannot *make people do anything*, I can still embrace these concepts in a broken world that rarely lives up to the expectations of the ideal in Scripture. With this knowledge, I can continue to aspire to be unified with the body of Christ, while realizing that a high degree of grace will need to be extended by me to others and for me from others, in order for this grand enterprise of unity to take shape as a reality.

DISCUSSION

1. Do you have trouble with the differences between the 'ideal' and the 'real' in life? Do you find yourself saying things such as "they *should* have done 'such and such'"; "they *ought to* do 'this or that'"?

2. When things don't go as they *should* go, do you drop out and quit? Or do you dig in deeper with a sense of conviction and graciousness?

3. When you realize that the human that is 'connected' to Christ as the body is also understood by the writer to be a soldier of Christ, how does this impact you and your understanding of Ephesians?

4. Do you think you have the energy and will to participate in the 'unity' of Christ's body, knowing that all of Christendom (and even Churches of Christ themselves) are so disjointed and not unified?

The Christian Spirit

Ed Gallagher

Focus Passage

Or do you not know that your body is a temple of the Holy Spirit within you, which you have from God, and that you are not your own? (1 Corinthians 6:19)

One Main Thing

The Spirit that dwells and works within the believer is God's Spirit.

Introduction

The Holy Spirit is mysterious. I think it's supposed to be that way. His purpose is not to tell us about Himself. Jesus told his disciples: "But the Advocate, the Holy Spirit, whom the Father will send in my name, will teach you everything, and remind you of all that I have said to you" (John 14:26). And again: "When the Advocate comes, whom I will send to you from the Father, the Spirit of truth who comes from the Father, he will testify on my behalf" (15:26). Rather than testifying about Himself, the Spirit testifies about Jesus. He reminds the disciples of Jesus about what Jesus has said. When the Spirit has done His work, the disciples of Jesus might not have a great understanding of the Spirit, but they will have a better understanding of Jesus.

C. S. Lewis suggests another reason that the Spirit might be less distinct than are the Father and Son.

> Do not be worried or surprised if you find it (or Him) rather vaguer or more shadowy in your mind than the other two. I think there is a reason why that must be so. In the Christian life you are not usually looking *at* Him: He is always acting through you.[1]

As Lewis says, we might think of the Father as in front of us and the Son as beside us while the Spirit is within us or behind us.

Though much of the life and work of the Holy Spirit is unclear to me, we can grasp some things from the evidence of Scripture. One of those things is what we just read from Lewis: the Spirit dwells within us. Paul's letters are especially insistent on this point, and especially Romans 8, the chapter in the New Testament with the most number of occurrences of the word "spirit." One example: "But you are not in the flesh; you are in the Spirit, since the Spirit of God dwells in you. Anyone who does not have the Spirit of Christ does not belong to him" (Romans 8:9). More on this later.

For now, what is this Spirit that dwells within Christian believers?

GOING DEEPER

The Greek word translated "spirit" is *pneuma* (πνεῦμα), appearing 379 times in the New Testament, including every book except 2–3 John. It mostly refers to God's Spirit (275x), but can also refer to the human spirit (e.g., Luke 8:55) or a demonic spirit (e.g., Luke 8:2, 29). The standard dictionary for the Greek New Testament discusses this word across four and a half pages, supplying eight different major definitions, starting with "air in movement."[2] The word sometimes means "breath" or "wind" (cf. Hebrews 1:7), which allows for the different nuances of the word in Jesus's speech to Nicodemus: "The *pneuma* (wind) blows where it chooses, and you hear the sound of it, but you do not know where it comes from or where it goes. So it is with everyone who is born of the *pneuma* (Spirit)" (John 3:8).

The relevant Hebrew word is similarly broad in meaning, but references to the divine Spirit are much less frequent in the Old Testament. Our word is *ruaḥ* (רוּחַ), and it appears 389 times in the Hebrew Bible,[3] but a rather low percentage of these appearances are in reference to God's Spirit (only about 75x). One of the standard dictionaries of ancient Hebrew uses thirteen pages to define this word,[4] but there are only three major definitions: wind, breath, and the divine Spirit.

While the Old Testament supplies crucial information about God's Spirit, especially its work of empowering people—Bezalel in his artistry (Exodus 31:1–5) or Samson in his feats of strength (e.g., Judges 14:6)—it is the New Testament that depicts the Spirit with greater clarity. According to the New Testament, the Spirit belongs in company with the Father and the Son. For example, Jesus commanded His apostles to baptize people "in the name of the Father and of the Son and of the Holy Spirit" (Matthew 28:19). Peter addressed his first letter to believers "who have been chosen and destined by God the Father and sanctified by the Spirit to be obedient to Jesus Christ and to be sprinkled with his blood" (1 Peter 1:2). Paul ended his second letter to the Corinthians with this blessing: "The grace of the Lord Jesus Christ, the love of God, and the communion of the Holy Spirit be with all of you" (2 Corinthians 13:14).[5] And, of course, among the seven Ones mentioned by Paul in Ephesians 4 are One God, One Lord, and One Spirit (Ephesians 4:4–6).[6]

These passages show that when one speaks of the Christian God, one should speak of not only Father and Son but also Spirit. Traditional Christian theology has pressed further, describing the Christian God as one essence in three persons.[7] While the Apostle's Creed and the original Nicene Creed (325 AD) included belief in the Holy Spirit as a fundamental doctrine, the expanded Nicene Creed (381 AD) elaborated somewhat on the Spirit's being and activities and the responsibility of believers to "worship and glorify" Him together with the Father and the Son.[8] The New Testament does not provide examples of Christians worshiping the Holy Spirit, but it does provide evidence—beyond the threefold descriptions of God reviewed above—that the apostles conceived of the Holy Spirit as God. A classic example is the twin statements from Peter in Acts 5, who first accuses Ananias of lying to the Holy Spirit (5:3), and then of lying to God (5:4). The divinity of the Spirit would also explain why Jesus regarded blasphemy of the Holy Spirit as such a serious offense (Mark 3:29). Christians in the early centuries considered it appropriate—necessary—to offer worship to the Spirit since He is God.[9] I myself have sung few songs directly addressed to the Spirit, but one such song I have sung many times in my life: "Spirit, we love you, we worship and adore you, glorify thy name in all the earth!"

There are also indications in Scripture that the Spirit is personal, that He has thoughts and desires and agency. Paul and Barnabas undertook the first missionary journey in the book of Acts because the Holy Spirit called them to that work and spoke about his choice (Acts 13:2). Larry Hurtado points especially to the Farewell Discourse in John's Gospel as offering such testimony about the Spirit. In this passage, the Spirit is depicted as an Advocate or Counselor (*parak-lētos*; John 14:26, 15:26, 16:7), a personal representative of Jesus (14:16–20), who will remind the disciples of Jesus's teaching (14:25–26, 15:26, 16:12–13), bring glory to Jesus (16:14), and rebuke the world for sin (16:7–11).

> This frequent use of verbs of agency has the effect of giving the Spirit a considerably more personal character than we find in the OT and the Jewish tradition of the time, in which the Spirit is often referred to in ways that can connote more simply a divine power/force (e.g. 1 Samuel 10:9–13).[10]

What about the Spirit's pronouns? If the Spirit is personal, does that mean we should refer to the Spirit as "He" and not as "It"? Many Christians insist on using the masculine pronoun for this reason. Others use the feminine pronoun, "she," which does, in fact, correspond to the grammatical gender of the word "spirit" in Hebrew (*ruah* is usually feminine). Look, gender is such a controversial topic in the twenty-first century that we run the risk of inserting modern categories and concepts into ancient and timeless texts by bringing up the issue. Without advocating for a particular approach, I will note a few facts. The Greek word for "spirit" is neuter, and neuter pronouns (i.e., "it") are sometimes used in the Greek New Testament in reference to the Spirit (John 14:17, Romans 8:16). Some modern believers think that masculine (or feminine) pronouns are too "human" for the Deity, who is beyond gender. And some believers do not use pronouns at all in reference to God, instead repeating the word "God" where others would use a pronoun. I myself tend to speak about the Spirit as "He," sometimes "It."

APPLICATION

"Your body is a temple of the Holy Spirit within you, which you have from God" (1 Corinthians 6:19). Other New Testament passages describe the believing community as God's temple (1 Corinthians 3:16–17, Ephesians 2:21–22, 1 Peter 2:5), but at the end of 1 Corinthians 6, Paul applied the image to the bodies of individual Christians. Perhaps Paul stole the idea from Jesus, who once referred to His own body as God's temple (John 2:21). Just as God's presence filled the tabernacle (Exodus 40:34–35) and Solomon's temple (1 Kings 8:10–11), the same is true for the body of Jesus (Colossians 2:9) and the Christian believer. The Holy Spirit—the presence of God—dwells within our bodies. God has marked us with His seal (2 Corinthians 1:22; Ephesians 1:13, 4:30), designating us as His territory. (A different image: He has planted His flag in us.) This is exactly the point Paul was making in 1 Corinthians 6. Because my body is a temple of the Holy Spirit, I do not belong to myself, but I have been "bought for a price," and as God's temple I should be bringing glory to God in my body (1 Corinthians 6:20). Since "no one will see the Lord" without sanctification (Hebrews 12:14), I should allow God's Holy Spirit within me to guide me toward holiness. That is what it means for God to be at work within me (Philippians 2:13).

CONCLUSION

We might not know as much about the Holy Spirit as we would like–or as much as we know about the Father and the Son—but this we can know, both from the New Testament and from early interpretations of the New Testament: the Holy Spirit is God. Moreover, the Holy Spirit dwells within us, so that we are temples for God, individually and collectively. This is both an incredible privilege and an incredible responsibility. God has claimed us as His territory; we should act like it.

DISCUSSION QUESTIONS

1. Why is the Holy Spirit more mysterious to many Christians than is the Father or the Son?
2. Is it important to think and talk about the Holy Spirit as God? Why?
3. What pronouns should believers use in reference to the Holy Spirit?
4. Should Christians worship the Holy Spirit? How should that worship be expressed?
5. How does the Holy Spirit contribute to your spiritual formation or sanctification?

ENDNOTES

[1] C. S. Lewis, *Mere Christianity* (London: Geoffrey Bles, 1952), within chapter 4.4, titled "Good Infection."

[2] Frederick William Danker, ed., *A Greek-English Lexicon of the New Testament and Other Early Christian Literature*, 3d ed. (Chicago: University of Chicago Press, 2000), 832–36.

[3] The number 389 includes eleven appearances of the Aramaic cognate within the Aramaic portions of Daniel.

[4] David J. A. Clines, ed., *The Dictionary of Classical Hebrew*, 8 vols. (Sheffield: Sheffield Phoenix, 1993–2011), 7.427–40.

[5] In some English translations (e.g., NRSV), this same verse is given the number 13 rather than 14. At any rate, it's the last statement of 2 Corinthians.

[6] Other passages that mention together Father, Son, and Spirit, are 1 Corinthians 12:4–6; Galatians 3:11–14. Some passages mention the Son and the Spirit (1 Corinthians 6:11; Hebrews 10:29).

[7] For an account of Trinitarian theology, see Gilles Emery and Matthew Levering, eds., *The Oxford Handbook of the Trinity* (Oxford: Oxford University Press, 2011), especially the article by Bruce D. Marshall, "The Deep Things of God: Trinitarian Pneumatology," pp. 400–413. I also appreciate the simple treatment of the Trinity by C. S. Lewis in the chapter of *Mere Christianity* already mentioned, called "Good Infection."

[8] For an excellent argument that the Churches of Christ ought to value such early theological statements, see Leonard Allen, *In the Great Stream: Imagining Churches of Christ in the Christian Tradition* (Abilene, TX: ACU Press, 2021)

[9] See, for instance, the way the fourth-century Greek theologian Gregory of Nazianzus treats the issue of worshiping the Spirit in his *Oration* 31.12.

[10] Larry W. Hurtado, *God in New Testament Theology* (Nashville: Abingdon, 2010), 80.

Only One Spirit?

Ed Gallagher

Focus Passage

If we live by the Spirit, let us also keep in step with the Spirit. (Galatians 5:25)

One Main Thing

The most important evidence for the presence of God's Spirit within a person is the manifestation of the fruit of the Spirit.

Introduction

A person without God's Spirit is not a Christian. The New Testament is clear on this point, particularly the apostle Paul. "Anyone who does not have the Spirit of Christ does not belong to him" (Romans 8:9). In his rebuke of the Christians in Galatia, he used the expression "received the Spirit" to mean "became a Christian." "Did you receive the Spirit by doing the works of the law or by believing what you heard?" (Galatians 3:2). Paul (1 Corinthians 12:13) agrees with Peter (Acts 2:38) that believers receive the divine Spirit at baptism. When Paul encountered a dozen disciples in Ephesus, he asked them about their experience of the Spirit. When he learned that they didn't have the Spirit, he knew something had gone wrong; it turned out that these people had not even been baptized into Christ (Acts 19:1–7).

A follower of Jesus must be one who honors and cultivates—does not quench (1 Thessalonians 5:19) or grieve (Ephesians 4:30)—the Spirit's work in his or her life. After all, that's what Jesus did. The Spirit descended upon Jesus at His baptism (Mark 1:10), and Jesus began His ministry by proclaiming Himself anointed by God's Spirit (Luke 4:16–20; cf. 4:1). It was the Spirit of God that empowered Jesus's ministry of exorcism (Matthew 12:28). Jesus rejoiced in the Spirit (Luke 10:21). The Spirit was involved in the resurrection of Jesus (Romans 1:4), just as He will be in ours (8:11). Jesus had no comforting words for someone who would blaspheme the divine Spirit (Mark 3:29).

Jesus told His disciples that they would be better off once He was no longer physically present among them. Can you imagine that? If we didn't know that Jesus Himself said it, we would declare such an idea undiluted hogwash. But Jesus said that His departure would be accompanied by the outpouring of the Spirit. "I tell you the truth: it is to your advantage that I go away, for if I do not go away, the Paraclete will not come to you; but if I go, I will send him to you" (John 16:7).

Going Deeper

The Holy Spirit makes intermittent appearances in the Old Testament. The particular term "Holy Spirit," in fact, shows up in only two passages (Psalm 51:11; Isaiah 63:10–11), but God's Spirit is mentioned several dozen times. Not only is the divine Spirit mentioned relatively infrequently in the Old Testament (compared with the New Testament), but there are indications that only select individuals benefited from the Spirit's presence, not the people of God generally. In one particularly telling passage, Moses expresses the wish that "all the Lord's people were prophets, and that the LORD would put his spirit on them" (Numbers 11:29). As the scholar Mark Boda has written,

> The dominant feature of OT pneumatology is that the Spirit of God appears to be restricted to covenantal leaders, whether leader (Deut. 34:9), elder (Num. 11:25), judge (Judg. 3:10), king (1 Sam. 10:6), or prophet (Zech. 7:12), but does not appear to indwell the community as a whole (Num. 11:29).[1]

The Hebrew prophets—particularly Joel 2:28–32—envision a future moment when this would all change, when God would "pour out my Spirit on all flesh." John the Baptist told the crowds of a coming one who would perform baptism in the Holy Spirit (Mark 1:8). In Acts 2, the apostle Peter announced that the promised outpouring of the divine Spirit had finally come to pass (Acts 2:16). And on the same day, he assured every baptized believer of the gift of the Holy Spirit (Acts 2:38).

As you know, dear reader, there are different ways of understanding these biblical statements about the Spirit. I think the easiest, most obvious interpretation is that every believer—every follower of Christ—from the time of Peter's proclamation and forever after—enjoys the presence of God in their lives through the Spirit that indwells them. Christians are God's temple (e.g., 1 Corinthians 3:16, 6:19), inhabited by God's Spirit. Are we talking about the personal presence of God's Spirit within the believer's body? That does seem to me the simplest understanding. If you think it best to understand these promises in a different way, fine—as long as we all affirm that "anyone who does not have the Spirit of Christ does not belong to him" (Romans 8:9).

APPLICATION

How do you know that a believer has the Spirit of Christ? One way of answering the question is to say simply, "The Bible says it. I believe it. That settles it." I like that answer, because I trust Scripture. But perhaps we can say more about the Spirit's work in our lives.

Here we encounter disagreements. The promise in Joel that we quoted earlier entails that "your sons and your daughters shall prophesy, your old men shall dream dreams, and your young men shall see visions" (Joel 2:28). Indeed, we find something close to this in the New Testament descriptions of the spiritual gifts distributed to believers. To be sure, there are visions and prophetic dreams described in the New Testament (e.g., Acts 9:10, 10:3, 16:9, 18:9), but these are not listed among the spiritual gifts enjoyed generally by believers (cf. 1 Corinthians 12:4–10). Instead, other gifts are mentioned: wisdom, knowledge, faith, healing, tongues, and more. In fact, Acts 2:17 is the only verse in the New Testament containing the word "dream" (ἐνύπνιον, *enypnion*). My point is that we should not press the language of Joel 2:28 too far; even in the earliest days of the church, when it was obvious that Joel's vision had—at least, partially—come to fulfillment, the details of that vision did not strictly apply. The Spirit was at work in a new way, just as Joel had promised, and the Spirit's activities exceeded Joel's imaginings.

What about supernatural gifts? A first-century Christian could say that they knew they had the Spirit of Christ, in part, because of the spiritual gifts they enjoyed. In Galatians 3:5, Paul essentially equated the reception of the Spirit with the working of miracles. And today the fastest growing segment of Christianity is charismatic, claiming to have received the empowering from God's Spirit to perform the same spiritual gifts that we read about in the New Testament. (The Greek word for "gifts" in 1 Corinthians 12:4 is χαρίσματα, *charismata*, whence the description "charismatic.") Some of these groups declare that the gift of tongues is the initial sign that one has been accepted by God.

I myself have not experienced these gifts, and neither have most of the Christians I know. Are we missing something? We should remember that when it comes to the spiritual gifts, it is the Spirit "who allots to each one individually just as the Spirit chooses" (1 Corinthians 12:11). According to Paul's primary account of the spiritual gifts, not everyone receives the same gift (1 Corinthians 12:4–10, 27–31), and no particular charismatic gift is the *sine qua non* of the Spirit-filled Christian.

In the same context, Paul does name a *sine qua non* of the Spirit-filled Christian. "If I speak in the tongues of mortals and of angels, but do not have love, I am a noisy gong or a clanging cymbal" (1 Corinthians 13:1). Without love, I am nothing (v. 2) and I gain nothing (v. 3). Love of God and of neighbor are the greatest commandments (Matthew 22:34–40), the fulfillment of the law (Romans 13:9–10), and the first of the fruit of the Spirit (Galatians 5:22).

Let me point out that the fruit of the Spirit is unlike the *charismata* (the spiritual gifts). The fruit of the Spirit are not "allotted to each one individually just as the Spirit chooses." The fruit are not gifts given to different believers. While Christians sometimes wonder about which gifts the Spirit has given them, and sometimes they take a spiritual gifts inventory, there is no need to wonder which fruit the Spirit is developing in me. The answer is: all of them. It's not that my fruit is peace and yours is self-control. No! When the Spirit indwells someone, the Spirit of Christ cultivates the fruit of the Spirit—the character of Christ—in that person. The Spirit cultivates love and joy and peace and patience and kindness and goodness and faithfulness and gentleness and self-control in that individual believer.

This is the primary, the fundamental, sign of the Spirit's presence. How do you know you have the Spirit of Christ? Spiritual growth, that's how. You become like Christ, which is the whole point of Christianity (Romans 8:29; Ephesians 4:15). The Spirit's work in you—always, for everyone—is the development of the Spirit's fruit. Are you more loving today than when you were baptized, or than a few years ago? Joyful? Patient? If not, you are quenching the Spirit, grieving him. It's time to dedicate yourself to prayer and meditating on Scripture, and service and corporate worship and other spiritual disciplines by which you can develop the soil of your heart (cf. Mark 4:1–9).[2] The Spirit, an excellent gardener, can grow his fruit in a prepared heart.

Conclusion

Without Christ's Spirit, you do not belong to Christ. Without the Spirit of adoption, you are not God's child (Romans 8:15–16). The primary work of the Spirit in the life of the believer is to accomplish the primary goal of the Christian: to become like Christ. This entails exhibiting love (just like Jesus), and joy (just like Jesus), and peace (just like Jesus), and patience (just like Jesus), and all the other fruit of the Spirit (just like Jesus). Your job is to open yourself to the Spirit's work by engaging in the spiritual disciplines of, among others, prayer and meditation on Scripture and Christian community. In this way, the One Spirit indwelling Christians binds us to Christ and to each other. This is how we "keep the unity of the Spirit in the bond of peace" (Ephesians 4:3).

Discussion Questions

1. What does it mean that the Holy Spirit dwells within believers?
2. What does the Holy Spirit do for believers today?
3. Does the Holy Spirit supply people today with the spiritual gifts that Paul discussed in 1 Corinthians 12? Why?
4. What fruit of the Spirit do you find easiest to display? Which is most troublesome?
5. What practices, habits, do you find most helpful —or most intriguing—for growing spiritually?

ENDNOTES

[1] Mark J. Boda, *The Heartbeat of Old Testament Theology: Three Creedal Expressions* (Grand Rapids: Baker, 2017), 180.

[2] See my essay "Corporate Worship as Spiritual Discipline," in *Approaching Christian Scripture Faithfully: Twenty Attempts* (Florence, AL: Cypress, 2023), 169–84. For an introduction to the spiritual disciplines, see John Mark Comer, *Practicing the Way: Be with Jesus; Become Like Him; Do as He Did* (Colorado Springs: Waterbrook, 2024).

The Christian Hope
W. Kirk Brothers

Focus Passage

Ephesians 4:1–6. [Scripture quotations are from the New American Standard unless otherwise noted.]

One Main Thing

"Where there is hope there is life" (Norman Vincent Peale).

Introduction

Dr. Norman Vincent Peale took the well-known saying, "Where there is life there is hope," and gave it a twist: "Where there is hope there is life." He went on to say, "You're never beaten down as long as you have hope" (*Guideposts.org*, "Stories"). Hope is at the heart of New Testament teaching and especially the teaching of the apostle Paul. The words of Paul while discussing the second coming of Christ in 1 Thessalonians 4 can serve to summarize Paul's perspective: "But we do not want you to be uninformed, brethren, about those who are asleep, so that you will not grieve as do the rest who have no hope" (1 Thessalonians 4:13). Let us dive into the term "hope" and how it was used in the New Testament.

Going Deeper

The noun "hope" (*elpis*) is found 53 times in the New Testament and 36 times in Paul's letters (three times in Ephesians). The verb form (*elpidzō*) is found 33 times in the New Testament and 19 times in Paul's writings. The related word *proelpidzó*, "the first to hope," is present one time in Scripture, in Ephesians 1:12. The words are used ten times in the book of Acts, and six of those uses are by Paul (thus meaning that Paul used the words 64% of the time they were used in the New Testament). He uses the words most often in the books of Romans (17 times) and 2 Corinthians (8 times). Next come 2 Corinthians (5 times), 1 Timothy (5 times), 1 Thessalonians (4 times), and Ephesians (4 times).

Hope was a key component in the three-part (sometimes two-part) formula summarizing the Christian life: faith, hope, and love. An example of this is 1 Thessalonians 1:3, where Paul speaks of "constantly bearing in mind your work of faith and labor of love and steadfastness of hope in our Lord Jesus Christ in the presence of our God and Father" (cf. also 1 Thessalonians 4:8; 1 Corinthians 13:13; Galatians 5:5–6; Colossians 1:4–5). The formula is also found in Hebrews 6 and 10, as well as in 1 Peter 1:21–22. Faith brings us into a relationship with Christ. Love summarizes how we live in Christ and embody Him in the world. Hope is what enables us to remain steadfast and strong in our faith despite struggles. Paul used the "hope" words four times in 1 Thessalonians and once in 2 Thessalonians. His reference to hope in 1 Thessalonians 1:3 was significant in light of the "afflictions" the Thessalonians were facing (cf. 1 Thessalonians 1:6; Acts 17). The theme phrase I use for 1 Thessalonians is "Serve Him now, see Him later." The theme verses I use are 1 Thessalonians 1:9–10. Paul writes the letter to . . .

1. Encourage them as they faced persecution.
2. Explain more clearly the second coming (38% of the book).
3. Exhort them to live godly lives and to correct wrong practices.

Hope was a key means of encouraging his readers, and it pointed them to the second coming of Christ. Hope refers to ***"the looking forward to something with reason for confidence respecting fulfillment"*** (*elpis* in BDAG). Hope sees beyond the physical to spiritual and eternal realities (cf. Romans 8:24–25; Hebrews 11:1). It is confident expectation of the future. Thus, Paul frequently spoke of looking forward with expectation to the return of Christ (cf. 1 Thessalonians 1:10; Titus 2:13).

This hope is based on the work of Christ and the promises of God. In the Roman letter Paul calls our heavenly Father the "God of hope" (15:13), and in 1 Timothy 4:10 he says we have fixed our hope in the "living God." Titus 1:2 states that we have the hope of eternal life because God, who promised it to us, "cannot lie." Thus, in spite of tribulations, Christians can live expectantly.

Though only found four times in the book of Ephesians, the concept of "hope" is still central. The theme verse for Ephesians is chapter 1, verse 3: "Blessed be the God and

Father of our Lord Jesus Christ, who has blessed us with every spiritual blessing in the heavenly places in Christ." The theme phrase I use for the book is "Blessed in Christ to Be Like Christ." The first half of the book focuses primarily on the blessings we have in Christ (chapters 1–3), and the second half of the book focuses on becoming like Christ (4–6). With verse 4 of chapter 1, Paul begins to highlight some of the blessings we have in Christ. In verses 10–12 he states, "In Him also we have obtained an inheritance, having been predestined according to His purpose who works all things after the counsel of His will, to the end that **we who were the first to hope in Christ** would be to the praise of His glory." "We" likely refers to Jewish Christians who were the first to become followers of Christ (cf. Acts 2:5). In chapter 2 he prays that "the eyes of your heart may be enlightened, so that you will know. . . ." He wanted their mental lights to come on so they could realize the blessings they already have because of Christ. These blessings included **"the hope of His calling"** (1:18). In chapter 2 he highlights their condition before and after Christ. He stressed that before Christ they had **"no hope"** because they were "without God in the world" (2:12; cf. 1 Thessalonians 4:13). We will talk about the use of hope in chapter 4 in the next chapter.

Application

Hope changes everything. We have already noted that Paul wrote 1 Thessalonians to Christians facing persecution who had questions and misunderstandings related to the second coming of Christ. They were so excited about the return of Christ that they were afraid that Christians who died prior to the return would miss out on the special event. Paul stresses in chapter 4 that they will not miss out; in fact, they will join Jesus before those Christians who are still alive when Jesus comes (1 Thessalonians 4:13–18). He leads into that section by saying, "But we do not want you to be uninformed, brethren, about those who are asleep, so that you will not grieve as do the rest who have no hope" (1 Thessalonians 4:13). Because of Christ we have "hope laid up in heaven" (Colossians 1:5). Thus, we can live "looking for the blessed hope and the appearing of the glory of our Great God and Savior, Christ Jesus" (Titus 2:13).

No matter what we face in life, no matter what we lose, no matter what people do to us . . . we have hope. Peter highlights this reality for us,

> Blessed be the God and Father of our Lord Jesus Christ, who according to His great mercy has caused us to be **born again to a living hope** through the resurrection of Jesus Christ from the dead, to obtain an inheritance which is imperishable and undefiled and will not fade away, reserved in heaven for you, who are protected by the power of God through faith for a salvation ready to be revealed in the last time. **In this you greatly rejoice, even though now for a little while, if necessary, you have been distressed by various trials** (1 Peter 1:3–6, emphasis mine).

Hope allows us to live differently. We need not despair. We can live looking up!

CONCLUSION

Life preservers are required on boats in most states. Commercial airplanes have inflatable life preservers and even life rafts on them in the event that a water landing is necessary in an emergency. What does a life preserver do? It brings the person wearing it back to the surface when they are submerged in the water. Hope buoys us back to the emotional surface when we are drowning in struggles and sorrow. Hope makes all the difference!

DISCUSSION QUESTIONS

1. What verse in this lesson was most powerful to you and why? Also, feel free to share other verses about hope that are not mentioned in this lesson but are meaningful to you.
2. Discuss the difference between facing death with God and facing it without God.
3. Discuss reasons why we tend to look down at our sorrows instead of looking up at our hope.
4. Discuss what it means to live "looking for the blessed hope and the appearing of the glory of our Great God and Savior, Christ Jesus."

Only One Hope?

W. Kirk Brothers

Focus Passage

Ephesians 4:1–6

One Main Thing

"Where there is hope there is life" (Norman Vincent Peale).

Introduction

A piece of diorite that was as tall as a 45-story building and weighing 770,000 tons broke free from a mountain in Chile and plunged through a mine dug into that mountain. Thirty-three miners found themselves trapped in an emergency refuge with very little food and water under the mountain. People from all over Chile and the world responded to try to save them. Families of the miners set up camp just outside the mine entrance to wait and pray. The makeshift camp was called "Campo de Esperanza" (Camp Hope). Our last lesson focused on "hope" in the New Testament and specifically in the writings and sermons of Paul. Now we consider the concept of "one hope" in Ephesians 4.

Going Deeper

The theme of Ephesians is "Blessed in Christ to Become Like Christ." We looked at Paul's use of "hope" in the first half of Ephesians in the last chapter. The emphasis in the letter shifts in Ephesians 4 from the blessings we have in Christ to the kind of people we should be because of those blessings. Part of being like Christ is being unified in love: "being diligent to preserve the unity of the Spirit in the bond of peace" (4:3). The Spirit had unified them. In chapter one Paul told them they were given the Spirit as a seal and a pledge/guarantee when they heard and believed the gospel, the message of truth (1:11–14; cf. "gift of the Holy Spirit" in Acts 2:38). First Corinthians 12:13 states, "For by one Spirit we were all baptized into one body, whether Jews or Greeks, whether slaves or free, and we were all made to drink of one Spirit." In chapter 2 of Ephesians, Paul revealed that Jewish and non-Jewish believers had been joined together in Christ, "in whom you also are built together into a dwelling of God in the Spirit" (2:22, cf. 1 Corinthians 16–17). Before Christ, if they visited the temple in Jerusalem, the Gentile readers of this letter were separated from the presence of God (Ephesians 2:11–13). After Christ's death, the dividing wall at the temple, which forbade Gentiles to cross, was symbolically broken (Ephesians 2:14), and now all Christians (Jew and Gentile) receive the Spirit and are brought together to become temples of the Spirit. Now God lives in them both, as one temple, one body.

Assuming that they realized that the Spirit had made all

believers one in Christ, Paul wanted them to be "diligent" to keep that oneness. The word "diligent" translates the word *spoudádzō*. It means "to be especially conscientious in discharging an obligation, be zealous/eager, take pains, make every effort" (BDAG[1]). The word implies rushing to act because of the importance of the task. Paul motivated them to keep this "oneness" in the Spirit, to be one in peace and love (cf. 4:1–14) by reminding them that "oneness" is at the heart of their relationship with God: One body, one spirit, one hope, one Lord, one faith, one baptism, and one God (4:5–6).

One of those "ones" is "one hope of your calling" (Ephesians 4:4). For Paul, hope was both a blessing from a Christ (as emphasized in chapters 1 and 2 of Ephesians) and a motivation to live like Christ in unity and genuine faith (the emphasis here in chapter 4). We focused on the hope that Christians have in the previous chapter. Now we need to delve into the concept of "one hope." How is it that we have "one hope," as opposed to many? There are many things that might give us hope as believers. What did Paul have in mind when he used the word "one" here? The full phrase is "just as you were called in one hope of your calling" (4:4). This is not the first connection between calling and hope in Ephesians. Remember that Paul was reminding the Ephesians of the blessings they have in Christ (cf. 1:3). The books of both Ephesians and Colossians seem to have as backdrops the danger of worldly teachings, philosophies, and beliefs being added to faith in Christ. Paul stressed that "all spiritual blessings" (not some, most, or many) are found in Christ (as opposed to anyone or anywhere else).

Newspaper publisher William Randolph Hearst invested a fortune in collecting art treasures from around the world. He had agents who helped him to purchase these works of art. On one occasion, he gave a list of items for purchase to one of his agents. The agent searched for months before returning to tell Hearst that he already owned the items, and they were in his warehouse. He did not realize what he already had (*Bible Exposition Commentary*, Vol 2, page 14). Paul wanted the Ephesians to realize what they already had, so they were not drawn to something or someone else. He wanted the Ephesians to have "the eyes of their heart enlightened" (Ephesians 1:18). Imagine the agent taking Hearst to his warehouse and turning on a light to show him the works of art he already owned. Similarly, Paul wanted the mental light to come on for his readers so they could see and remember what they had in Jesus. He highlights three things he wanted them to know, and the first of those is "the hope of His calling" (1:18).

Paul stressed throughout his writing that believers (in fact, all people) are called by God through the gospel/good news (2 Thessalonians 2:14; cf. Ephesians 4:1; Colossians 3:15; 2 Timothy 1:9; 1 Thessalonians 2:12, 5:24). Paul told the Colossians that they heard about their hope through the preaching of the gospel by Epaphras (Colossians 1:5–7). The idea of calling is a reminder that God acts first in our salvation. We do not cause our salvation. We respond. Furthermore, this calling is a calling of hope.

"So that you will know what is the hope of His calling . . ." (1:18).

"Just as you were called in one hope of your calling . . ." (4:4).

Paul uses the definite article ("the" in English, i.e., "the hope") in Ephesians 1:18 (cf. the same in Colossians 1:5, 23, 27). He may be talking about a specific hope.

So what is the "one" hope Paul is referring to? I spent so much time reminding us of the purpose of Paul's letter to the Ephesians because I believe it is the key to unlocking the significance of there being "one" hope. The letter focused on all spiritual blessings being found "in Christ" (Ephesians 1:3). This includes hope. We are called through the preaching of the good news/gospel (2 Thessalonians 2:14; Colossians 1:5–7). Jesus is the heart of the good news (1 Corinthians 15:1–11). Peter declared in Acts 4:10 that a lame man was raised "by the name of Jesus Christ the Nazarene" (cf. Acts 3:1–14). He then went on to say, "And there is salvation in no one else; for there is no other name under heaven that has been given among men by which we must be saved" (Acts 4:12). Peter also wrote that we are "born again to a living hope through the resurrection of Jesus Christ" (1 Peter 1:3). In Ephesians 1 Paul spoke of being among the first "to hope **in Christ**" (1:12, emphasis mine). Paul summarized the mystery he preached as "Christ in you, **the hope** of glory" (Colossians 1:27, emphasis mine). This is consistent with Ephesians 2 where Paul said that previously the Ephesians had "no hope and [were] without God in the world" (2:12). He then stated, "But now in Christ Jesus you who formerly were far off have been brought near by the blood of Christ" (Ephesians 2:13). For me, it seems clear that the New Testament teaches that Jesus Christ is the one hope. Paul confirms this in 1 Timothy 1:1 when he refers to "Christ Jesus, who is our hope."

APPLICATION

As we reflect on Christ as our one hope, there are three points of application that come to my mind. The first point of application is that we need to give Jesus our sins. There is salvation in no other name. If anyone has not expressed his or her faith through repentance of sins, confession of faith in Christ, and baptism in the name of the Father, the Son, and the Holy Spirit, he/she needs to do so immediately. Secondly, we need to give Jesus ourselves and live in faithful obedience to Him. Paul told the Romans that hope that does not disappoint grows out of proven character (Romans 5:4). He challenged the Colossians to "continue in the faith firmly established and steadfast, and not moved away from the hope of the gospel" (Colossians 1:23). Finally, we need to sell others on our Savior and be "ready to make a defense to everyone who asks you to give an account for the hope that is in you, yet with gentleness and reverence" (1 Peter 3:15).

CONCLUSION

On day 17 of their ordeal, a small drill finally made it down to where the miners were. That tiny, 4 ½ inch hole, 2,300 feet underground, became their lifeline until they were finally rescued after 69 days because of special technology made possible, in part, by NASA. The families had patiently waited in Camp Hope for two months. When miners began to emerge one by one, people exploded in celebration. Their hopes and dreams had come true.

This life is not easy. We will face struggles, heartaches, and disappointments that can bury us in despair. Yet, because of Christ, we can pitch our tents in "Camp Hope" and wait patiently for the freedom and celebration laid up in heaven.

Discussion Questions

1. What verse in this lesson was most powerful to you and why?

2. Discuss what it must have been like for the miners trapped in that mine for 69 days.
3. Discuss how their story can help us think about our situation before Christ.
4. What was your most important takeaway from this chapter?

ENDNOTE

[1] BDAG—Frederick William Danker, ed., *A Greek-English Lexicon of the New Testament and Other Early Christian Literature*, 3d ed. (Chicago: University of Chicago Press, 2000), 832–36.

THE CHRISTIAN LORD

MICHAEL D. JACKSON

INTRODUCTION

When someone calls my wife "the boss," especially in the South, it has a humorous and playful ring to it. We associate "the boss" with earthly leaders who are our direct authorities in our workplace, so the metaphor carries the connotation that I "report directly to her" in my other areas of life. Many of us have some familiarity with the nature and purpose of metaphors—to show a strong comparison even though something isn't literally true. Whether or not my wife is actually "the boss," the metaphor conjures a picture that is easy to see.

I think that sometimes people think that the concept of "Lord" is also a metaphor when applied to Jesus. They may have heard of "lords and ladies" from medieval Europe, seen a play or movie, and immediately make the connection of Lordship with the words they read in Scripture. After all, we don't have "lords" today, and the usage of the term has fallen out of favor for the most part in American English.

Is the term "Lord," as applied to Jesus Christ, a

metaphor? Strong comparison notwithstanding, it is not. It is a literal role of our savior and deserves our attention.

DIGGING DEEPER

When Paul refers to Jesus as "Lord" in Ephesians (see Ephesians 1:2, 1:3, 1:15, 1:17, and many, many more), the title is more than a metaphor. Deeply rooted in both a religious context and the historical context of the day, "Lord" connotes a serious title for Jesus with deep and lingering effects on our lives.

It is widely recognized that in the time of the New Testament, Jews had generally begun avoiding pronouncing the name of God from the Hebrew Scriptures (YHWH). Philo and Josephus both speak of the importance of avoiding speaking God's personal name. The Mishnah later assumes that the prohibition is well-established.

What many may not know is that the chosen replacement for God's personal name in the Greek translation of the Hebrew Scriptures (the Septuagint) was *kurios*. This Greek word is the same word applied to Jesus repeatedly in the Greek New Testament. English readers might miss the connection, but to a Greek reader, there is at minimum a backdrop in which the name of God is associated with the concept of "Lordship" that is ascribed to Jesus.

Additionally, in the secular Greco-Roman context, "lords" were *owners*. For instance, in Matthew 10:24, when Jesus says that "A disciple is not above his teacher, nor a slave above his *master*," it is unfortunate that we can't see the original language at work here. Our word, *kurios*, is the word translated "master." A *kurios*/owner in the New Testament could refer to an owner of a vineyard, house, harvest, or sabbath ... but also an owner of people. Slave masters were "lords."

Imagine this imagery intertwined when Paul introduces himself in another letter as "the slave of Christ Jesus." As he opens Ephesians (and other of his letters), Jesus is paired with God in the common formula of "God the Father" and "Our Lord Jesus Christ." Far from a metaphor, this title of Jesus indicates the deity of Jesus and our conscription to Him as the one who owns us as Christians.

The visual of the Lordship of Christ is captured in several phrases in Ephesians. Paul says Christ is "seated at God's right hand in the heavenlies" (1:20), that He is "far above all rule and authority and power and dominion, and every name that is named, not only in this age but also in the one to come" (1:21), and "head over all things to the church" (1:22). Ephesus was clearly a place of intense interest in spiritual powers, magic, and mysticism (see the "book burning" in Acts 19:19). Paul is sure to situate the Christian Lord as far above all of these powers, deserving rightful rulership over all of creation, including you and me.

Many writers have noticed in our text in Ephesians 4:4–6, Paul says that there is both "One God" and "One Lord," a striking resemblance to the Shema of Deuteronomy 6:4 that says "Hear, O Israel: The LORD our God, the LORD is one." Paul affirms that there is only one God, while simultaneously ascribing deity and lordship to Jesus within this monotheistic framework.

Jesus's lordship should be understood in light of His explicit teaching on the matter in the New Testament. James and John, the two sons of Zebedee, sought out Jesus in Mark 10:35ff in order to make their requests of Him for when "He came into His glory." Their desire? To sit on His right hand and His left hand. Jesus sharply questions them, not about their leadership ability, nor their education, nor their power or authority. He asks them if they are able to "drink the cup that I drink." His lordship is born out of service and suffering, not "lording over."

He teaches the disciples (and us) an incredibly valuable lesson on what His lordship actually looks like. "You know that those who are recognized as rulers of the Gentiles lord it over them; and their great men exercise authority over them." (Mark 10:42). "But it is not this way among you ... whoever wishes to become great among you shall be your servant ... For even the Son of Man did not come to be served, but to serve, and to give his life as a ransom for many" (Mark 10:43).

The same Lord who washed His disciples' feet as He was on the cusp of betrayal by one of those very disciples is the Lord who is now ruler over our lives. Our voluntary yielding of our lives to Him is not purely because of His power and authority and dominion, though all those things are important. Rather, it is His desire to give of Himself (everything) on our behalf that especially qualifies Him to take our full allegiance and servitude.

APPLICATION

The End of Autonomy

The primary application of Christ's lordship in our lives is the death of personal autonomy. Modern Western culture idolizes the "self-made man" and the autonomy of the individual will. The confession "Jesus is Lord" is a voluntary surrender of that autonomy. If He is Lord, the believer is not. As Paul argues in 1 Corinthians 6:19–20, "You are not your own, for you were bought with a price."

This application hits home in the area of decision-making. The question for the Christian is never "What do I want to do?" but "What does the Lord want me to do?" (Ephesians 5:10, "Try to discern what is pleasing to the Lord"). The lordship of Jesus invades every sphere: career choices, financial management, sexual ethics, and time usage. To call Him Lord while retaining control over these areas is a contradiction in terms. This is a point Jesus Himself made: "Why do you call me 'Lord, Lord,' and not do what I tell you?" (Luke 6:46).

Lordship in the Home

Ephesians provides a specific application of lordship in the domestic sphere in Ephesians 5:21–6:9. Paul radically reorients the Roman household around the lordship of Jesus.

- Wives and Husbands: Submission is done "as to the Lord" (Ephesians 5:22).
- Children and Parents: Obedience is "in the Lord" (Ephesians 6:1).
- Slaves and Masters: Service is rendered "as to the Lord and not to men" (Ephesians 6:7).

The application here is penetrating: Christ as our Lord mediates every human relationship. A wife submits to her husband not because the husband is ultimate, but out of reverence for the Lord. A slave works hard not because the earthly master deserves it, but because the slave is actually serving Christ. This transforms mundane labor into divine obedience. It also checks the power of authority figures. The master cannot abuse the slave because the Master also has a Lord in heaven who shows no partiality (Ephesians 6:9). The "One Lord" levels the playing field, making everyone a fellow servant under the same King.

Baptism as Allegiance

The connection in Ephesians 4:5 between "One Lord," "One Faith," and "One Baptism" suggests that baptism includes within it a public picture of allegiance to Christ as our Lord in faith. An application can be drawn for the modern church regarding the seriousness of baptism. In addition to being God's commandment for the remission of our sins, it is also the putting on of the uniform of the Lord's army. It marks the believer as "property of Jesus." In a culture of fluid identity, baptism into the "One Lord" provides a fixed, eternal identity. We are those who have called upon the name of the Lord.

DISCUSSION QUESTIONS

1. Redefining Power: In Ephesians 1:20–23, Jesus is described as having authority over all "rule, authority, power, and dominion." How does Jesus's definition of "lordship" (marked by self-giving love and service) differ from the world's definition of power? How should this affect the way we lead in our families and workplaces?
2. The Name Above Every Name: Paul claims Jesus has the name above every name. What are the "names" or "powers" in our modern world

that try to assert authority over us? How does the present lordship of Jesus help us withstand these influences?

3. The Functional Lord Test: It is easy to call Jesus "Lord" on Sunday. What specific areas of life are the hardest for you to submit to His lordship on Monday? What does "resistance" in those areas reveal about our hearts?

4. Master in Heaven: Read Ephesians 6:5–9. Paul tells earthly masters that they have a "Master in heaven" and that He shows no partiality. How does this truth change the way we treat others and interact with them?

Only One Lord?

Michael D. Jackson

Introduction

In the South, it is common for "a coke" to function intentionally as the same thing as "a soda," or as would be called in some places, "a pop." It is quite possible to ask someone for "a coke" or to "bring cokes" to a fellowship meal, and you may end up with a Coke, Coke Zero, Pepsi, or even a Sprite. The marketplace is represented by a singular product that has come to represent the entire genre of fizzy drinks.

The ancient world was hyper-religious, contrary to what our intuition may tell us, due to the often-rampant hedonism in many ancient cultures. Paul himself says

> For even if there are so-called gods whether in heaven or on earth, as indeed there are many gods and many lords, yet for us there is but one God, the Father, from whom are all things and we exist for Him; and one Lord, Jesus Christ, by whom are all things, and we exist through Him. (1 Corinthians 8:5–6, NASB95)

Trade guilds, cities, and even families all had their patron deities. Over time in the Roman Empire, the emphasis on what is called the "Imperial Cult" added an additional layer, where subjects of the Roman Empire publicly performed obeisance through festivals, sacrifices, incense offerings, vows, and temple patronage tied to the emperor and "Rome." In this pluralistic society, to claim that there was "Only one Lord" was an act of cultural push-back and political subversion. It was this very claim that led Christians to be called "atheists" in accusations by their counterparts in culture. The refusal to pay homage to the traditional gods and bow to Caesar led to persecution.

The significance of the "One" in Ephesians 4:5 is its unifying power. It is a simple comparison, but imagine if "coke" really meant "Coke." There is only one thing that is being referenced. Now, imagine if there are not "lords" but really only "One Lord." There is only one Sovereign over the cosmos and only one church over which He is the head. The single "Lord" smashes the walls of division that exist between Jew and Gentile, slave and free.

Digging Deeper

Ephesus is well known for its connection with Artemis/Diana (Acts 19). The Temple of Artemis was one of the Seven Wonders of the Ancient World that dominated the landscape and economy of the city. In Acts 19, Paul's preaching sets off a riot sparked by the fear that it would discredit the goddess "whom all Asia and the world worship" (Acts 19:27). She offered protection, prosperity, and identity. The claim that there is "One Lord" confronts the culture that built up Artemis as a very real figure of power in the community. In short, the claim for "One Lord" is a direct claim of Artemis as fiction, unable to deliver on the promises everyone had believed for so long. The people of Ephesus walked by the Temple of Artemis on a regular basis. The claim that a Jewish carpenter who was crucified by Rome was the "real Lord" required boldness, faith, and courage. Jesus was the cornerstone (see Ephesians 2:20–22) that rendered the Temple of Artemis obsolete.

The worship of the Roman Emperor, as mentioned above, was a growing force in Asia Minor in the middle of the first century. Nero, and later Domitian, adopted titles like "Lord" and "God." Some authors claim that the Christian confession of "One Lord" was an intentional and direct co-opting of imperial language to rebel culturally against the Empire. The result would be that Caesar's authority was derived, limited, and subject to judgment. The ultimate allegiance of the human soul is to Jesus, not the state.

The "One Lord" of Ephesians 4:4–6 is notably the "center" of the Seven Ones:

One Body, One Spirit, One Hope, **ONE LORD (Center)**, One Faith, One Baptism, One God and Father

The Lord Jesus is the mediator at the heart of Paul's thinking.

Perhaps one of the greatest core theological concepts that Paul is arguing with the "One Lord" language is the reconciliation of Jews and Gentiles in Christ. In the ancient mindset, gods were territorial and ethnic. Israel had Yahweh, but other peoples and places had their own deities for obeisance. If Jesus were merely "for a tribe," He could be the Lord of the Jews, and Gentiles could stick with their own deities.

Paul's argument is that because God is One and there is One Lord, the distinction between Jew and Gentile is abolished (Ephesians 3:6). The universal Lord means there is a universal church. He is the "peace that broke down the dividing wall" (Ephesians 2:14). If there is only One Lord, then everyone must be under the same reign.

Application

Modern Idolatry

While we may not have the Temple of Artemis, Calvin said that the human mind is an "idol factory." The claim of only One Lord is as counter-cultural today as it ever has been. Idols are things that absorb your heart and imagination more than God; anything you seek to give you what only the Lordship of Christ in your life could give you.

If pressure or circumstances lead you to follow something other than Christ, it can be argued that those things are truly your lord. If your career demands you compromise your integrity, and you do it, then your career is your Lord. If lust pulls you away from your faithful commitments to God or your spouse, then sex is your Lord. If the acquiring of power leads you to step on or over others in pursuit of your selfish ambition, then your ambition is your Lord.

Political Tribalism

In our very polarized society (at least here in the United States), politics can sometimes overtake an individual's allegiance to the "One Lord." When our opinions are more important than our moral convictions, this too can be problematic. I understand that our moral convictions can be the basis of our political convictions, so this is not what I'm referencing here. It is just important to remember that the

"One Lord" unites all of us based on our theological convictions first and foremost.

The Unifying Power of Submission

Returning to the analogy in the introduction: when "coke" can mean anything, the term loses its specific power. If "Lord" can mean Jesus *plus* my political party, or Jesus *plus* my career ambitions, the term loses its unifying power.

Paul emphasizes "One Lord" in Ephesians to smash the walls of division. Why? Because when two people are fully submitted to the same Master, they cannot be at war with one another. Discord in the church often arises because we have competing "lords." One person is serving the lord of "Traditionalism," another is serving the lord of "Progress," and another is serving the lord of "Personal Preference."

When the "One Lord" is truly Jesus, the ground is level: The Jew and Gentile, the slave and free. Or, in our context, the rich and poor, the Boomer and the Gen-Z, all find unity not because they agree on everything, but because they submit to the same King. The "One Lord" aligns us. If I am bowing to Jesus, and you are bowing to Jesus, we are, by definition, looking in the same direction.

The Ultimate Question

The application of this text forces us to look in the mirror and ask the difficult question: *Is He actually Lord?*

It is easy to sing "He is Lord" within the safety of an auditorium. It is much harder to live it when the commands of the Lord conflict with the desires of the flesh or the pressures of the culture. The ancient Christians in Ephesus disrupted their economy and risked their lives to insist there was only One Lord. Does our confession cost us anything? If our "Lordship" looks exactly like the world's "freedom," we may have simply renamed our own desires "Jesus."

Let us strive to be a people where "Lord" is not a generic title like a southern "coke," but the specific, defining reality of our existence. He is the One. There is no other.

Discussion Questions

1. The Exclusive Claim: In our pluralistic society, the claim that there is "Only One Lord" and "One Way" is often seen as arrogant or intolerant. How can we communicate this truth with "gentleness and respect" (1 Peter 3:15) without compromising its exclusivity?

2. Identifying Idols: Tim Keller suggests that an idol is whatever you feel you must have to be happy. What are some common "functional lords" in our community or culture that compete with Jesus for our ultimate affection? How do we practically dethrone them?

3. Politics and Lordship: How does the reality of "One Lord" affect the way we engage in politics? If Jesus is the only true Lord, how should that change the way we speak about political leaders or opponents?

4. Unity in Diversity: Paul used the "One Lord" to unite Jews and Gentiles. These groups had strong animosity towards each other. Who are the groups today that the church struggles to unite? How does focusing on the "One Lord" help bridge those divides?

THE CHRISTIAN FAITH
NATHAN DAILY

FOCUS PASSAGE

Hebrews 10:22–23; 11:1–3

... let us draw near with a sincere heart in the assurance that faith brings, because we have had our hearts sprinkled clean from an evil conscience and our bodies washed pure in water. And let us hold unwaveringly to the hope that we confess, for the one who made the promise is faithful.

Now faith is the substance of what we hope for, being convinced of what we do not see. For by it the people of old received God's commendation. By faith we understand the worlds were set in order at God's command, so that the visible has its origin in the invisible.

INTRODUCTION

The biblical concept of faith should not be understood as solely equivalent to belief. Many popular phrases, including "leap of faith," "keep the faith," "blind faith," "unquestioning faith," and "have a little faith," just to name a few, have led some, even many, practitioners toward defining faith in terms of an uncritical and unreasonable acceptance of or a belief in matters unknown. In the Bible, faith is a broader term than belief, a concept that includes not only belief but also knowledge and action. As we will see, faith[1] includes not only faith in a God (belief) but also placing faith in that God (trust), being faithful to a God (obedience) who is also faithful (divine promise), and being a member of the faith (community) who lives the faith (as modeled by God and Jesus) and practices the faith (doctrine).

As the terms in the Old Testament and New Testament that are translated as or related to faith occur several hundred times in a variety of contexts, faith defies any simplistic definition.[2] Most helpful are those definitions that accentuate various components of meaning derived from the diverse contexts in the biblical canon where the words translated "faith" are used. For example, faith connotes "the entire human response to God, including belief, trust, obedience, endurance, and loyalty. It is a response of the whole person,"[3] or faith includes "persuasion, conviction, and commitment, and always implies confidence, which is expressed in human relationships as fidelity, trust, assurance, oath, proof, guarantee."[4]

Going Deeper

The numerous biblical texts that appeal or allude to faith provide a resource for creating a broad and vibrant definition of the concept. Many narratives, laws, covenants, poems, and letters present faith with a variety of forms and illustrations both positive and negative (Genesis 12–22; Exodus 4; Deuteronomy 28; 1 Kings 2; 2 Kings 17, 21;

Isaiah 49; Zecheriah 8; Psalms 19, 40, 78, 89, 119; Daniel 1–6; Nehemiah 9; 2 Chronicles 31–32; Matthew 8–9; 24; Luke 8; John 1–21; Acts 13; Romans 1, 3–4, 10; Galatians 3; Ephesians 1; Colossians 2; 1 Thessalonians 3; 1 Timothy 1–6; Hebrews 1, 11; James 2). From the many examples, a few texts will explore avenues for inquiry into the nature of biblical faith.

Faith as a human response receives definition through modeling by God. The Torah begins to apply the term faithful to the God of Israel in those generations after Abraham. As the characters of the Torah recognize God's promises to Abraham taking hold (Genesis 12, 15), they appeal to the God of Abraham as one who is faithful (Genesis 24:27). When God responds to the idolatry of Israel at Sinai (Exodus 32–34), faithfulness appears as a key component of God's character. God states in Exodus 34:5–7, "The LORD, the LORD, the compassionate and gracious God, slow to anger, and abounding in loyal love and faithfulness." These words form a core definition of the character of God that is alluded to throughout the Bible (Numbers 14:18; Nehemiah 9:17; Psalms 86:15, 103:8–13, 145:8; Joel 2:13; Jonah 4:2; Micah 7:18; Nahum 1:3; 2 Chronicles 30:9). Appearing as a component of God's self-definition after the episode of the golden calf, faithfulness becomes an aspect of God's response to idolatry and, thus, making promises on behalf of and choosing Israel to be God's own people is central to God's character. The New Testament presents a similar conviction, "if we are faithless, he will remain faithful, for he cannot disown himself" (2 Timothy 2:13). The God who is faithful to Israel becomes the subject of Israel's praise (Deuteronomy 7:9, 32:4; Isaiah 49:7; Psalms 33:4; Lamentations 3:21–23; 1 Corinthians 1:9) and, ultimately, a model for replication by a faithful people (Joshua 24:14, 1

Samuel 12:24).[5] When faith is articulated as a human response of trust and obedience toward the divine one, faith is not blind but is a reaction to the character and actions of God whereby humans may learn to replicate a posture for life modeled by the God who is faithful (Philippains 2:1–11; Revelation 14:12).

Faith as a divine response arises from promise to provide impetus for trusting the divine one. Insofar as human faith is modeled from divine character, divine faithfulness bolsters trust that all the promises of God will come to fruition. In Genesis 12, God promises Abram not only descendants but a great nation that will be constituted by the blessing of God. In Exodus 4, with the people of Israel now in Egyptian slavery, God and Moses discuss the faith of Israel, a faith that is confirmed upon God's deliverance of the people (Exodus 14:31). Upon entering the land, now a great nation (Deuteronomy 26:5), Israel affirms that all of God's promises have come to completion (Joshua 21:45). These promises are the reason Israel may trust or have faith in God. In the promised land, God provides David a new promise (2 Samuel 7). This great nation (7:23–24) will remain great permanently under the leadership of the Davidic house. God promises David that his house will "stand" (i.e. be established, faithful, lasting; 7:16), and David responds by praying that God's words remain "true" (i.e., faithful; 7:28). As the word for faith appears twice in 2 Samuel 7, biblical authors appeal to God's eternal promise for a Davidic house as an indicator of God's own faithfulness toward Israel (1 Samuel 25:28; 2 Samuel 23:5; 1 Kings 11:38; Isaiah 7:9; 1 Chronicles 17:23ff; 2 Chronicles 1:9, 6:17) and express confidence that God will act on behalf of the promise when the Davidic monarchy falls (Psalms 89; Isaiah 49:7; 55:3; cf. 1 Kings 8:26).[6] The biblical story of

God's promises toward Israel provides a foundation for faith because God's attention to these promises throughout Israel's history points to a God who can be trusted to remember and act for Israel (Exodus 2:24; Nehemiah 9; Psalms 78, 105–106). Thereby, God's people may live in faith in expectation that God will continue to work on their behalf in an ongoing manner.

The faith of Jesus Christ appears as a tangible action on behalf of humanity that enhances knowledge of God, proves God's care, and becomes the source for all faith. In the book of Galatians, Paul tells the readers that they are justified, that is "declared in the right or placed in the right relationship with God," because of the faith of Jesus Christ, that is "Jesus Christ's act of fidelity in undergoing death for our sake."[7] Again, faith must not be solely equated with belief as the faith of Jesus Christ becomes manifest in death, that ultimate moment when Jesus was faithful to God (Galatians 1:4, 2:20–21; Romans 3:3, 21–22, 25; 4:25; 5:8; 1 Corinthians 6:11).[8] To emphasize the importance of the faith of Jesus Christ for the people of God, Paul turns to the story of Abraham to state that Abraham was viewed as right before God because of the faith/trust he placed in God (Galatians 3:6; Genesis 15:6) and to the teaching of Habakkuk to state a life of being right with God is founded upon faith (Galatians 3:11; Habakkuk 2:4). Just as Abraham's reaction to God's message and God's answer to Habakkuk's lament is faith/trust, Paul encourages the people of God to understand that faith, that is Jesus's faith exemplified in death on a cross, is the mark that they are justified or made right before God or may be called children of God (Galatians 3:23). Here faith is an event. The people of faith are those who craft their identity upon that event, the death of Jesus, and hold no other event in comparison

(Galatians 5:6). That God loved humanity and demonstrated that love through Jesus as "we were still sinners" (Romans 5:8) is confirmation of God's faithfulness and a definition of the faith God's people espouse.

APPLICATION

The well-known definition of faith in Hebrews 11:1 provides a fitting conclusion: *Faith is the substance of what we hope for, being convinced of what we do not see.* Faith is connected to hope, but again, this is not a blind hope. Faith is not what one makes up when there is nothing to see. As Hebrews 10:23 notes, hope derives from knowing "the one who has made the promise is faithful." As a *substance*, faith is that part that makes real for "right now" (the "already") what is hoped for in the future (the "the not yet"). As we have seen, in the faith of Jesus Christ, we have access to that substance or part (faith) which provides us with an understanding of what "will be," even though, for now, what "will be" is currently unseen.[9] Faith, defined and exhibited in the death of Jesus, is a substance we already have (knowledge of Jesus's act on our behalf) that allows us to know the reality of what we do not yet see. Faith is grounded in promise, trust, and confidence that God has worked in this world and, those of us who are God's people, know that God will continue to do so as "every one of God's promises are "Yes" in [Jesus Christ]; therefore, also through him the "Amen"[10] is spoken" (2 Corinthians 1:20).

DISCUSSION QUESTIONS

1. How have you defined faith? How do the scriptural texts in this chapter help you add to your definition of faith? Choose any one of the scriptures cited above to read. Discuss how the verse(s) helps you better understand the concept of faith.

2. Why is "belief" only a partial or insufficient definition of faith?

3. How is God faithful? How can humans be faithful? Why should humans have faith?

4. Discuss the key components of the character of God in Exodus 34. Why does God choose to embody these characteristics?

5. How is obedience central to the definition of faith (Revelation 14:12)?

6. What do biblical authors teach God's people about faith when it seems that God's promises are not being kept?

7. Compare translations of Galatians 2:16. How is the translation "faith of Jesus Christ" different from "faith in Jesus Christ"? How does Paul relate the "faith of Jesus Christ" to the death of Jesus and to the faith of God's people?

8. How can prayer be a declaration of faith?

9. Insofar as we receive our definition of faith as faithfulness is modeled by God and Jesus Christ, how might we enact and model faith (as more than belief) in the contexts where we live?

ENDNOTES

[1] For a discussion of the nature of faith as a religious concept, see John Bishop and Daniel J McKaughan, "Faith," in *Stanford Encyclopedia of Philosophy*, eds. Edward N. Zalta and Uri Nodelman (Stanford: Metaphysics Research Lab Stanford University, 2023), URL = https://plato.stanford.edu/archives/win2023/entries/faith/.

[2] See the treatments of *pistis* and *ʾāman* in R. W. L. Moberly, "אָמַן (*ʾāman* I)," *NIDOTTE* 1:421–27; Ceslas Spicq, "*pistis*," *TLNT* 3:110–116.

[3] Luke Timothy Johnson, *The Creed: What Christians Believe and Why It Matters* (New York: Doubleday, 2003), 44.

[4] Spicq, "*pistis*," *TLNT* 3:110.

[5] This section follows Moberly, "אָמַן (*ʾāman* I)," *NIDOTTE* 1:423.

[6] H. Wildberger, "אמן *ʾmn* firm, secure," *TLOT* 1:134–57.

[7] Richard B. Hays, "Galatians," *NIB* 11:235–48.

[8] Hays, 240; J. Louis Martyn, *Galatians: A New Translation with Introduction and Commentary* (AYB; New Haven: Yale University Press, 1997), 251–52, 263–74.

[9] See Luke Timothy Johnson, *Hebrews: A Commentary* (NTL: Louisville: Westminster, 2006), 278.

[10] Note that the word amen is based on a Hebrew word (*ʾāman*) deriving from the same root as the word translated "faith." Thus, the amen in 2 Corinthians 1:20 constitutes a statement of trust or confidence in the promises of God. Concluding prayer with "amen" is a theological statement, a statement of faith (truly, so be it). See, Moberly, "אָמַן (*ʾāman* I)," *NIDOTTE* 1:421–27

Only One Faith?

Nathan Daily

Focus Passage

From Paul ... to ... the faithful in Christ Jesus.

For he chose us in Christ before the foundation of the world that we should be holy and blameless before him in love.... when you heard the word of truth (the gospel of your salvation)—when you believed in Christ—you were marked with the seal of the promised Holy Spirit...

For this reason, because I have heard of your faith in the Lord Jesus and your love for all the saints, I do not cease to give thanks for you when I remember you in my prayers. I pray that the God of our Lord Jesus Christ ... will give you spiritual wisdom and revelation in your growing knowledge of him, ... so that you can know what is the hope of his calling ... and what is the incomparable greatness of his power toward us who believe, as displayed in the exercise of his immense strength. This power he exercised in Christ when he raised him from the dead and seated him at his right hand in the heavenly realms far above every rule and authority and power and dominion and every name that is named, not only in this age but also in the one to come. (from Ephesians chapter 1)

INTRODUCTION

Occupying the fifth place in the series of ones (Ephesians 4:4–6) is *one faith*. Mentioned 12 times in the letter, faith occupies a position of central concern through the entirety of Ephesians (1:1, 13, 15, 19; 2:8; 3:12, 17; 4:5, 13; 6:16, 21, 23). A summary of the letter's 12 examples of the language of faith, provides a resource for qualifying the connotation of "one faith" in 4:5.

The letter is addressed to the "faithful in Christ Jesus" (1:1) who have placed their faith or trust in Christ upon becoming sealed in the Holy Spirit (1:13). Reports of this faith have now come to Paul (1:15); therefore, he consistently gives thanks for them in his prayers (1:16). In his prayer, Paul appeals to the power of God displayed in the resurrection that is now available to the faithful (1:19–20). Upon responding to God's salvation in trust or faith, God's people receive God's gracious gift (2:8).[1] This grace of God brings enlightenment to all people so that the mystery of God's plan is disclosed (3:1–13). Paul's readers now have access to God because of Jesus's own faithfulness displayed on the cross (3:12). In a return to intercessory prayer, Paul prays that through faith the church may gain power from the Spirit whereby the Messiah will dwell in your hearts (3:16–17). Upon the onset of the covenantal relationship with God, the heart of the faithful will change so that Christ's own faith is displayed through the faithful.[2]

One faith, then, is listed among the seven ones of the

letter for the church to seek unity and exhibit the bond of peace (4:1–6). Achievement of unity is possible as a result Christ's gift who, following his ascension, has enabled apostles, prophets, evangelists, shepherds, and teachers to serve the holy ones, the body of Christ, until unity of faith is achieved (4:13). To remain strong and resist evil during the process of living and seeking unity, Paul depicts a series of metaphors for spiritual battle, the armor of God, which conclude with the shield of faith that extinguishes the flaming arrows of the evil one (6:16). This is the full body shield (*thureos* or *scutum*, 4' long x 2.5' wide) which indicates that faith or trust in God functions as a barrier from the multiple attacks from evil[3] as the people of God seek to walk in a manner worthy of the calling (4:1).

The letter concludes with reference to the faithful servant, Tychicus, who will interpret the letter and Paul's situation for the reader (6:21). The final reference to faith in the letter places faith alongside love and peace as being from God (6:23). Again, the ideals of the faithful Christian life precede Christian action by initially appearing as gifts from God.[4]

GOING DEEPER

Whereas the meaning of "one faith" is not elaborated in 4:5 but occurs in a list of seven items essential for unity among the people of God, the 12 references to faith throughout both sections of the letter provide a beginning point for considering what constitutes "one faith."

The language of one faith provides God's people with an understanding their own essence, that is as faithful ones, identified as and growing because of the work of Christ, that is the faith of Christ. We are faithful because we trust that

God is faithful. The letter of Ephesians is structurally divided into two sections: chapters 1–3 and chapters 4–6. Flowing from Paul's prayer in chapter 1 that the church may grow in knowledge of God (1:17), the first three chapters concentrate on presenting questions of the nature of God to the church: Who is God? What has God done? Teaching the commandments for Christian life appear in chapters 4–6, only following the depiction of God and God's grace in chapters 1–3. Knowing God is the initial and essential component that must precede commandment. The Christian life must be lived based on and in response to the God who offers life. Therefore, the second section of the book begins with the admonition "to live a life worthy of the calling with which you have been called" (4:1). The language of faith appears throughout both sections of the book. By referring to the readers as the faithful at the beginning of the book (1:1, 13, 15, 19), their status as loyal, trusting, faithful believers is established before the imperatives for living the Christian life commence (4–6). Faith is not a work (2:8) but is the trust in God's gift. Here, "[f]aith involves the abandonment of any attempt to justify oneself and an openness to God which is willing to accept what he has done in Christ."[5] In fact, deeming the readers as faithful results from their unity with God through Christ Jesus. Christ, who is the anointed one, is the prime example of faithfulness (3:12) who now dwells within the hearts of the readers through faith (3:17). These texts indicate that faithfulness was exhibited at the cross and continues to be exhibited through the heart of the believer. Both are works of God on behalf of the believing community. Those who trust that God through Jesus is faithful are now themselves labeled faithful and given gracious gifts to enact faithfulness. Now they will continue to emulate Jesus's faithfulness[6] by enacting the "one faith" until unity, knowledge, and maturity are realized (4:5, 13). Unity was initialized by the blood of Christ (2:13) and will continue as the readers emulate Jesus's example of unity (4:3, 13). Following instructions for walking in a manner worthy of the calling will produce continual growth toward this goal.

The language of one faith reminds God's people that the source of faith resides in the one God, revealed in the faith of Christ, for the benefit of maintaining promise to God's one people. A central theme of Ephesians is the mystery or divine secret recently revealed to the people of God (Ephesians 1:9; 3:3, 4, 9, 5:32; 6:19). This mystery is God's plan to unify all things in Christ (1:9–10). This unity is achieved through the death of Christ (2:11–13), whereby humans are incorporated into a body with Christ as head (1:10, 1:22–23). Insofar as Christ's death is for the benefit of all humanity, a key component of the mystery is that the dividing wall between Jews and Gentiles is destroyed so that all God's people are unified (2:11–22). This is not a new people of God. Rather, Gentiles are incorporated into as heirs into the one people of God (3:3–6).[7] The promises to God's people flow from the one God of Israel (Deuteronomy 6:4–5). In Genesis 12:1–3, God promises Abraham that "all families of the earth will be blessed though" him. Ephesians sees this mystery as solved in the blood of Christ where both Jews and Gentiles are unified, in fulfillment of God's promise to God's people (Ephesians 2:12, 3:6), as "fellow citizens" of "God's household" who will together form a dwelling place for God (2:22)[8] just as the temple formed a dwelling place for God (2 Samuel 7:14). Because of Christ's faithfulness to death on behalf all humans (1:7; 2:13), the mystery or divine secret is that through this act God has chosen to provide a path for unity among all people and ultimately all creation (1:9–10). As one people unified in loyalty to one God, one faith must be present among all of them, one faith defined by and through the faith of Christ.

APPLICATION

In Ephesians, faith appears as a disposition of trust toward God, a gift from God through Spirit and Christ Jesus, a path toward unity, a cosmic force for protection from evil, and an element of the character of God that works toward the ultimate goals of life that reveal God's work in the world. The faith is "one" because it shares and replicates the faith of Christ and because it is a faith of one people in one God, a God who has gained trust through compassion and love for a people. Thereby, the faithful in Ephesians are ones who experience the power of God, the power that raised Jesus from the dead, so that they may initiate the peace, love, and unity of God to the world as they learn and begin to walk in a manner worthy of the calling (4:1).

DISCUSSION QUESTIONS

1. Read the verses on faithfulness in the book of Ephesians. What is the meaning of faith in these verses? How is faith illustrated and conceptualized in these verses? What other biblical texts help define faith similarly to the examples in Ephesians?
2. How is faith more than belief in the book of Ephesians?

3. Should faith be considered a work (2:8)? Why or why not?

4. How is Ephesians structurally divided into two sections? Find examples in each section that help reveal this structure.

5. Since one faith is a sign of unity (4:1–5), what is the nature, character, and content of one faith?

6. How does the story of Abraham's faith relate to the faith of the church? How is this faith only one faith?

7. How might the faith of Christ help us define one faith that unifies God's people (Ephesians 4:1–6; Romans 3:22; Galatians 2:16; 2:20; Ephesians 2:8, 3:12)?

ENDNOTES

[1] For discussion of the various interpretation issues present in 2:8, see David A. DeSilva, *Ephesians* (NCBC; Cambridge: Cambridge University Press, 2022), 122–25.

[2] Andrew Lincoln, *Ephesians* (WBC; Grand Rapids: Zondervan, 1990), 204; DeSilva, *Ephesians*, 181. See also, Markus Barth, *Ephesians 1–3: Introduction, Translation and Commentary on Chapters 1–3* (AYB; New Haven: Yale University Press, 1974), 370.

[3] Lincoln, *Ephesians*, 449.

[4] Lincoln, *Ephesians*, 468.

[5] Lincoln, *Ephesians*, 111.

[6] N. T. Wright, *The Vision of Ephesians: The Task of the Church and the Glory of God* (Grand Rapids: Zondervan, 2025), 15.

[7] David A. deSilva, *An Introduction to the New Testament: Contexts, Methods & Ministry Formation* (2d ed;

Downers Grove: IVP Academic, 2018), 931–35; Luke Timothy Johnson, *The Writings of the New Testament: An Interpretation* (3d ed; Minneapolis: Fortress, 2010), 366–67.

[8] Johnson, *Writings of the New Testament*, 367–68.

The Christian Baptism

Justin Guin

Focus Passage

"One Lord, one faith, one baptism" (Ephesians 4:5, ESV).

One Main Thing

Baptism connects the body to Christ and is foundational to unity.

Introduction

In Ephesians 4:1–16, Paul stressed the importance of maintaining unity in the church. Christ has effected spiritual unity through the cross. Both Jew and Gentile alike are made into "one body" (2:16) and are now under Christ's authority (1:23). Paul challenged the church to walk in a manner that is worthy of the gospel (4:1; cf. Philippians 1:27; 1 Thessalonians 2:12). This command begins with a change of attitude towards one another. Sin levels the playing field, and without Christ, you are without hope.

This is a motivating factor. Recognizing this fact should produce a sense of humility and servitude, and a willingness to fulfill one's role in helping the church grow (4:16).

Following this exhortation, Paul lists seven biblical fundamentals that provide the foundation for unity in the church (Ephesians 4:4–6). Each item in the list is preceded by the word "one," emphasizing its importance. The sixth item in this list is baptism. The church was baptized into one body through the Spirit (cf. 1 Corinthians 12:13). It was a shared experience during their conversion. When Paul arrived in Ephesus, he connected with a group of believers who were only familiar with John's baptism. As he taught, he asked whether they had received the Holy Spirit, and, to the apostle's surprise, they did not know who the Holy Spirit was. Paul corrected their understanding concerning baptism. John's baptism was in preparation for Jesus's ministry and emphasized repentance. Paul preached to them the gospel in its fullness. The Ephesians acted on this new teaching: "On hearing this, they were baptized in the name of the Lord Jesus. And when Paul had laid his hands on them, the Holy Spirit came on them, and they began speaking in tongues and prophesying" (Acts 19:5–6). This experience was a unifying event for the congregation since it was the final step in their conversion.

The church in the twenty-first century has a similar experience. Christ quelled sin's hostility and brought peace (cf. 2:12–13). Consequently, we are God's people built upon the foundation of the gospel (cf. 2:19–20). Baptism is a unifying point for every Christian and remains one of the seven pillars just as it did for the Ephesian church. Baptism connects the body to Christ and is foundational for unity. Therefore, we must understand this biblical practice.

GOING DEEPER

The word "baptism" in its various forms occurs seventy-three times in sixty verses in the English Standard Version. Danker defines it as "the ceremonious use of water for the purpose of renewing or establishing a relationship with God; plunging, dipping, washing, water-rite, baptism."[1] Purification through water was common in the Old Testament. A Jew must submit to ritual washings for many things that made one unclean (cf. Leviticus 11–13, 17:15, 22:4–6; Numbers 19:10–13, et al.). Furthermore, purifications were expected during times of sacrifice and temple worship. During the Second Temple period, Jews immersed Gentiles who converted to Judaism. This practice represented repentance and removed any hint of ceremonial uncleanness. So, baptism for conversion and spiritual cleansing was common by the time of Jesus.

The first occurrence of baptism is in Matthew 3:1, referring to John, who was known as "the Baptizer." As noted in the introduction, he preached a baptism of repentance in preparation (Mark 1:4). His message called on the Jews to prepare their hearts and to spark spiritual revival in anticipation of the coming Messiah. Still, it did not convert anyone to Christianity. Beginning in Acts 2, the practice of baptism changed due to the effect of the death, burial, and resurrection of Jesus. What changed, and why is baptism a part of God's plan of salvation?

Baptism and Forgiveness

In Acts 2, Peter preached the Gospel in its fullness for the first time. Jesus's ministry was according to the definite plan and foreknowledge of God (Acts 2:22–23). Peter provided scriptural proof for Jesus's death, resurrection, and lordship. As he concluded his sermon, he stated in Acts 2:36, "Let all the house of Israel therefore know for certain that God has made him both Lord and Christ, this Jesus whom you crucified." This statement was not just factual. It demanded a response, and the crowds recognized it because they asked, "What shall we do?" (v. 37). Peter responded in 2:38, *"Repent and be baptized every one of you in the name of Jesus Christ for the forgiveness of your sins, and you will receive the gift of the Holy Spirit."* Through Jesus's name, repentance and baptism took on a new meaning. The preposition "for" denotes purpose. Forgiveness is defined as the release of a formal obligation or debt, especially understood as the debt of sin.[2] The removal of sin prepares you for receiving the gift of the Holy Spirit.

In Acts 22, Paul recounts his conversion before the Jewish leadership. In Acts 22:16, Ananias commanded the apostle, *"And now why do you wait? Rise and be baptized and wash away your sins, calling on his name."* Paul must respond to Christ's initiative in his life. The commands were simple and understandable. Paul's eyes were opened both physically and spiritually when his sins were washed away. The whole process is described as "calling on the name of the Lord." This reference is the second time this phrase is linked to baptism and obeying the plan of salvation (cf. Acts 2:21, 37–38). Paul obeyed the same plan of salvation as Christians do today.

Since baptism forgives sins, it is essential to salvation. On this point, Peter wrote, "Baptism, which corresponds to this, now saves you, not as a removal of dirt from the body but as an appeal to God for a good conscience, through the resurrection of Jesus Christ" (1 Peter 3:21). Baptism corresponds with the flood waters during Noah's day (1 Peter

3:20) which removed the effects of sin from the earth. Baptism is not a ceremonial cleansing. It is obedience that connects you to the resurrection of Jesus. Which leads to the next point concerning baptism; it connects you to Jesus.

Baptism and the Connection to Jesus

In Galatians 3:27, the New Testament connects baptism in the believer's life to Christ. Paul wrote, *"For as many of you as were baptized into Christ have put on Christ."* Putting on Christ unites you with Jesus and clothes you with Jesus. In Romans 6:3ff, Paul further explains the spiritual effect this has on a Christian's life. Baptism crucifies the old man by being united in the death of Jesus. Then, a Christian shares in the resurrection and is raised to walk in newness of life (v. 4–5). Therefore, sin no longer rules the day in a Christian's life. Sin has lost its power, and you're free from its damning consequences (vv. 6–7).

In the Colossian letter, Paul wrote something similar to them. In Colossians 2:11–12, Paul likens baptism to circumcision and being buried in Christ. The resurrection is made possible by the "powerful working of God" (v. 12). We are no longer dead in sin. Through this act of obedience, you are made alive in Christ, having your sins forgiven (v. 13). Spiritual transformation is possible through baptism because it connects you to Jesus.

APPLICATION

Baptism is an act of obedience that all Christians experience. Submission to God's plan of salvation changes the eternal direction of one's life. It is how one becomes a disciple of Jesus (Matthew 28:19). Note a few points of application.

Baptism is a decision to submit to Christ, made after learning the gospel. In every conversion account in Acts, submitting to baptism is preceded by hearing the gospel and developing faith. The three thousand at Pentecost (Acts 2:37–38), the multitudes in Samaria (Acts 8:11–12), the Ethiopian (Acts 8:35–38), Cornelius's household (Acts 10:48), Lydia (Acts 16:11–15), the Philippian Jailer (16:25–33), and the Ephesians (Acts 19:1–5) all learned the gospel and rendered obedience. In the New Testament, no one is ever converted by a miraculous event. It occurred when another Christian shared the message of Jesus, and submission to the plan of salvation followed.

Baptism is the first step in a lifetime of obedience. Romans 12:1–2 reminds you of the continual transformation a Christian undergoes after baptism. You are expected to be a living sacrifice offered to God in submission to the gospel. Furthermore, Paul explains that the indwelling of the Holy Spirit demands holy living. You receive the Holy Spirit at baptism (Acts 2:38), and His presence is a seal of salvation (Ephesians 1:13–14). In light of this fact, Christians must be holy in daily life and seek to glorify God (1 Corinthians 6:19–20).

There is much misunderstanding concerning baptism in the religious world. A study of the New Testament helps you understand why Paul included it in his list of seven foundational principles. "One baptism" clothes you with Christ, where a wealth of spiritual blessings abound (Ephesians 1:3).

DISCUSSION QUESTIONS

1. What are the key scriptures related to baptism in the New Testament? How do these verses contribute to our understanding of its significance?
2. What is the primary purpose of baptism? How does it reflect a believer's commitment to their faith and community?
3. How do Acts 2:21, 38, and Acts 22:16 help you understand the meaning of "calling on the name of the Lord"?
4. Can you share your own baptism experience or your thoughts about the moments leading up to it? What emotions or thoughts did you have during that time?
5. How can the act of baptism influence a person's day-to-day life as a follower of Christ? In what ways does it serve as a reminder of one's faith journey?

ENDNOTES

[1] William Arndt et al., in *A Greek-English Lexicon of the New Testament and Other Early Christian Literature* (Chicago: University of Chicago Press, 2000), 165.

[2] Logos Bible Sense Lexicon, (Bellingham: Logos Bible Software) n.p.

Only One Baptism?

Justin Guin

Focus Passages

"One Lord, one faith, one baptism" (Ephesians 4:5, ESV).

"On hearing this, they were baptized in the name of the Lord Jesus" (Acts 19:5).

One Main Thing

While the term baptism is used in various ways in the New Testament, "one baptism" refers to being baptized in the name of Jesus for the forgiveness of sins.

Introduction

A unified church is a growing church, and the apostle emphasized unity in the letter to the Ephesians. Paul reminded them that every Christian has been saved through the gospel (Ephesians 1:3–8). Christ is their cornerstone (2:20), and working together leads to growth in every aspect

(4:16). In Ephesians 4:4–6, Paul listed seven pillars on which the unity of the church is built. In v. 5, he states there is "one baptism." A study of the New Testament shows a broad use of the word "baptism." How can there be only one baptism with such a variety of usage? Furthermore, to which baptism does this phrase refer?

In this chapter, we will note some of the different uses of the term "baptism." In our study, we will note how these occurrences differ from what the Ephesians obeyed in Acts 19:5. This analysis seeks to ascertain what Paul meant by "one baptism." While the term baptism is used in various ways in the New Testament, "one baptism" refers to being baptized in the name of Jesus for the forgiveness of sins.

Going Deeper

This word in its various forms is found seventy-three times in sixty verses in the English Standard Version. Danker defines it as "the ceremonious use of water for the purpose of renewing or establishing a relationship with God; plunging, dipping, washing, water-rite, baptism."[1] In the Old Testament, water purification was common and symbolized ritual purity (cf. Leviticus 11–13, 17:15, 22:4–6; Numbers 19:10–13, et al). In later Judaism, it was practiced by converts to Judaism, washing away the defilements of their Gentile, pagan past. So, by the time John the Baptist preached to the multitudes and commanded baptism, this practice was familiar to first-century Palestinian Jews.

The Baptism of John the Baptist

The Old Testament prophets foretold one who would prepare the way of the Messiah. The angel told Zechariah that his son would prophesy in the spirit of Elijah (Malachi 4:6) and would turn the hearts of Israel towards wisdom. His mission would be one of preparation (Luke 1:16–17). All four evangelists record John self-identifying as the one who cried in the wilderness to prepare for the coming Messiah (Matthew 3:3; Mark 1:3; Luke 3:4–5; John 1:23; citing Isaiah 40:3). Note how Mark summarized his mission, "John appeared, baptizing in the wilderness and proclaiming a baptism of repentance for the forgiveness of sins" (1:4). In the follow verse, he notes that multitudes were going out to him to be immersed.

Could this be the "one baptism" that Paul is referring to in Ephesians? Acts 19 seems to prove otherwise. Paul traveled to Asia Minor on his third missionary journey. When arriving in the city, he found some disciples and asked, "Did you receive the Holy Spirit when you believed?" As the conversation progressed, the apostle learned they were not disciples of the Lord. They had never heard of the Holy Spirit, much less received him. Thus, Paul clarified for them, "John baptized with the baptism of repentance, telling the people to believe in the one who was to come after him, that is, Jesus" (Acts 19:4). Upon hearing this message, the Ephesians were baptized "in the name of the Lord Jesus."

Both Mark and Paul reveal that John's baptism prepared those for the coming Messiah. Acts 19:2 further reveals that one did not receive the Holy Spirit upon obedience to John's message. Such was a marker of conversion (Acts 2:38; cf. John 3:3–5; Romans 8:9; et. al.). This account is not the only time someone is corrected who only knew John's baptism. In the verses preceding Acts 19, Apollos preached passionately and eloquently. Note one detail Luke wrote at the end of Acts 18:25, "Though he only knew the baptism of John." Priscilla and Aquila took him aside and accurately explained to him the "way of God." Given what we know from the text, this presumably is about his misunderstanding of baptism. Only through baptism "in the name of Jesus" can one transition from a disciple of John to Jesus. Thus, John's baptism cannot be the "one baptism" referenced in Ephesians 4:5.

The Baptism of Jesus

While different from conversion, John's baptism was vitally important in the gospel narratives. Could this account be what Paul is referring to by the phrase "one baptism"? Let's note Matthew's account of Jesus's baptism. In Matthew 3:13–15, Jesus came to John to be immersed by John (v. 13). Why would he need to be baptized by John if he baptized others for the remission of sins (Mark 1:4)? After John refused, Jesus explained, "Let it be so now, for thus it is fitting for us to fulfill all righteousness" (v. 15). What does this mean? Craig Blomberg summarized, "To fulfill all righteousness means to complete everything that forms a part of a relationship of obedience to God."[2] Fulfilling righteousness becomes a theme in Matthew's gospel from this point forward. Jesus blazed the path for His disciples to follow.

Jesus's obedience does a couple of important things. First, he validates John's message as a divine mandate for Israel to obey. Furthermore, it marks the first of two incidents in which Jesus received heavenly approval for his mission (v. 17; cf. Matthew 17:5). Although a significant event in the New Testament narrative, it does not appear to be connected to Paul's phrase "one baptism." It is not connected to the conversion of Christians as you find in Acts and in the Epistles.

The Baptism of the Holy Spirit

In Acts 1:5, Jesus foretold, "For John baptized with water, but you will be baptized with the Holy Spirit not many days from now." This prophecy was also foretold by John the Baptist (Matthew 3:11; Mark 1:8; Luke 3:16; John 1:33). There are two instances in which people were baptized with the Holy Spirit. First, in the days following Jesus's ascension, the Holy Spirit came upon the apostles in Jerusalem (Acts 2:1–2). The twelve were enabled to communicate in unstudied languages as they preached the gospel. These men were Galileans, and the Pentecost crowd noted their background. Note Acts 2:8, "And how is it that we hear them in our own language in which we were born?" (LSB) This miracle, brought about by the outpouring of the Spirit, proved that something divine was occurring in this account. Thus, Peter quoted Joel 2:28–32, noting that this event fulfilled Old Testament prophecy.

A second time occurred in Acts 10 when Peter taught Cornelius and his household the gospel. As Peter preached, the Spirit came upon them, enabling them to speak in tongues (10:44–46). This outpouring preceded their water baptism (10:47). When Peter later summarized this event, he concluded, "And as I began to speak, the Holy Spirit fell upon them as He did upon us at the beginning" (11:15). When was the beginning? It would be a reference to Acts 2.

So, at Pentecost and with Cornelius, the baptism of the

Holy Spirit was not essential for salvation. The apostles were already followers of Jesus, and the centurion and his family were later immersed in the name of Jesus (10:48). What was the purpose of the outpouring of the Spirit? Mark Moore sums it up well, "Thus, the only two times the New Testament identifies the baptism of the Holy Spirit, it was not for salvation but *validation*" (emp. added).[3] It proved the apostles were acting on the Christ-given mission to preach the gospel. For Cornelius and his household, it demonstrated that these Gentiles were bona fide converts to the gospel. The message transitioned from being only for Jews to the entire world (1:8). Thus, it seems unlikely that this is the "one baptism" referenced in Ephesians 4:5.

APPLICATION AND CONCLUSION

Unity requires a shared experience, and it is one thing that all seven items listed in Ephesians 4 have. All of the Christians in Ephesus were baptized "in the name of Jesus" (Acts 19:5). This phrase is synonymous with Jesus's authority (Acts 3:6, 16; 9:27; 16:18; 1 Corinthians 1:10; 6:11; Colossians 3:17; 2 Thessalonians 3:6). This principle is consistent with further New Testament teaching. Note a few points of application.

1. Baptism in the name of Jesus is consistently connected to conversion. Acts 2:38 is a well-known passage and the first occurrence of this principle. By Jesus's authority (v. 36), we are granted forgiveness and the indwelling of the Spirit after we're baptized. This message is consistently preached elsewhere in Acts (Acts 8:12, 16; 10:48; 19:5).

2. Baptism connects the church to Jesus and
    unifies us all under the banner of the gospel.
    Baptism buries the old person of sin, and we live
    as a new creation (Romans 6:1–6; 2 Corinthians
    5:17). It is more than a ritual cleaning. It is a
    powerful demonstration of God's work through
    the resurrection of Jesus (Colossians 2:12; 1
    Peter 3:21).

3. Baptism is used in other passages to encourage
    unity in the church. The Corinthian church
    was marked by schism. Paul pleaded with them
    to be unified "by the name of our Lord Jesus
    Christ" (1:10). Then he reminded them of their
    baptismal experience, "For by one Spirit we
    were all baptized into one body, whether Jews
    or Greeks, whether slaves or free, and we were
    all made to drink of one Spirit" (12:13). Note
    the parallel concepts with the seven ones of
    Ephesians 4—one Spirit, one body, and one
    baptism.

While the term baptism is used in various ways in the
New Testament, "one baptism" refers to being baptized in
the name of Jesus for the forgiveness of sins. It is a shared
act that all Christians experience. The twenty-first-century
church would do well to focus on this concept, too. All
Christians are connected to Jesus through obedience to the
gospel. Baptism connects us to Jesus and the Spirit. No one
is an exception. We are made one body by one Spirit who
gave one faith by the authority of one Lord and Father who
gave the one calling to submit to one baptism.

Discussion Questions

1. How do passages such as Colossians 3:17, Acts 16:18, and 1 Corinthians 1:10 help us understand the meaning of "in the name of Jesus"?
2. Contrast Acts 8:14–17 and 19:6–7 with the Spirit's baptism in Acts 2 and 10. What is the significant difference in how the Spirit came upon them? How does this show you that Acts 2 and 10 are unique events?
3. What was the purpose of the baptism of the Holy Spirit?
4. How does reflecting upon one's baptismal experience encourage unity?
5. What are some other ways the term baptism is used in the New Testament that were not discussed in this lesson? Consider Luke 3:16–17; Mark 10:35–40; and 1 Corinthians 10:1–2.

Endnotes

[1] William Arndt et al., in *A Greek-English Lexicon of the New Testament and Other Early Christian Literature* (Chicago: University of Chicago Press, 2000), 165.

[2] Craig Blomberg, *Matthew* NAC (Nashville: Broadman & Holman, 1992) 81.

[3] Mark Moore, *Acts* (Joplin: College Press, 2011), 53.

THE CHRISTIAN GOD

ANDREW PHILLIPS

Imagine you are in a boat that runs aground on a deserted island. As you wade across the sandy beach, you see a storm on the horizon. You immediately seek shelter. After what seems like an hour, you stumble upon a simple, well-built hut with a thatch roof. As you enter, you see a large cot on one side, along with a make-shift table and chair on the other. The table holds a stack of fruit, and one corner contains a few items that have clearly washed up on shore over the years. What would you assume? You would likely begin looking for the person who lives there. After all, the hut had to have some kind of cause, and its design shows you this was not thrown together by random chance. You would notice the items inside and see evidence of another person.

This scene provides a basic illustration of some enduring principles: the cosmological and teleological arguments for the existence of God. An easy way to remember them is the Cause/Effect Argument and the Design Argument. Like the imaginary hut in the story, our earth shows evidence of creation (it had to get here somehow) and of design (it sustains human life). For centuries, people have considered the world and reasoned that there must be someone or something that created it all. Paul draws on this principle in Romans 1:20, noting that since the beginning of creation, God's eternal power and divine nature have been seen through "the things that have been made." The creation around us points to a Creator.

But once we have determined there is a God, how do we decide which one? It is one thing to say there was a cause for creation. After all, many people believe that. But how can we know the cause was the God we read about in scripture?

ONE GOD

The Bible begins with a simple sentence: In the beginning God created the heavens and the earth. As we read that in the 21st century, we are struck by the powerful claim that our world did not just happen. It was created by God, which runs counter to many ideas in contemporary culture. The original audience for Genesis 1 would also have been struck by this powerful claim, but likely for a different reason. Many cultures in the ancient world believed in a pantheon of gods, and to assert there was only one would have run counter to their worship practices.

Centuries later, the same principle was true in Ephesus. When Paul writes to the Christians in Ephesians 4 about One God, this would have been a radically counter-cultural idea. The city of Ephesus was home to temples for Artemis, Apollos, Roma, Zeus, and even the emperor Augustus (since emperor worship was also encouraged in the Roman Empire).[1] The original readers of Ephesians would have grown up in an environment where worship of many gods was not only common but expected. We can imagine Christians in Ephesus who had friends and even family members who still worshipped regularly in those temples.

Preaching only One God rather than many threatened the way of life in Ephesus. To worship the true God on the throne meant "de-throning" every other pretender. Acts 19 gives us insight into this tension, as a silversmith named Demetrius speaks to a crowd of other workmen, saying,

> And you see and hear that not only in Ephesus, but in almost all of Asia, this Paul has persuaded and turned away a great many people, saying that gods made with hands are not gods. And there is danger not only that this trade of ours may come into disrepute, but also that the temple of the great goddess Artemis be counted as nothing, and that she may even be deposed of her magnificence, she whom all Asia and the world worship (Acts 19:26–27, ESV).

Centuries later, the same principle holds true in the 21st century. In an increasingly pluralistic culture, the idea of saying there is only one true God can be viewed as narrow-minded or even intolerant. Not only that, but there are competing idols in life that aren't religious in nature but demand that same kind of attention and devotion. This makes it tempting for us to settle for a faith that includes worship of God as one of many authorities in life, not the one and only. We will need the same kind of commitment the church in Ephesus needed to hold on to our faith in one true God.

THE CHRISTIAN GOD

In a world with so many competing gods, how can we know the God of the Bible is the one and only God, and how can we share that with others? Three important principles from the New Testament give us guidance.

The Incarnation of Jesus

In Philippians 2:5–11, Paul details how Jesus humbled Himself to come to earth as a human being. This is hard to imagine but important to understand: Jesus emptied Himself of His heavenly position to become human. This also sets the teaching of Christianity apart from other world religions. There were Greek and Roman mythological tales about gods pretending to be human, often in order to trick others, but Jesus took on flesh to bless others. There were other gods in the ancient world who demanded sacrifice, but only the true God of the Bible provided the ultimate sacrifice. The incarnation shows the extent God was willing to go to for us.

From a historical perspective, the existence of Jesus on earth has been clearly corroborated, and not just in the writings of Christians. In fact, two ancient authors, Tacitus (a Roman historian) and Josephus (a Jewish historian), clearly confirm several facts about Jesus. They tell us that Jesus existed, His personal name was Jesus, and He was called *Christos* in Greek; He had a brother named James; He won over both Jews and Greeks, the Jewish leaders looked down on Jesus, and Jesus was executed by crucifixion under the governorship of Pontius Pilate.[2]

Not only did Jesus walk the earth, but His teaching was distinct from other historical religious figures. For example,

Buddha claimed to show people the way to a noble life, but Jesus stated that He is THE way (John 14:6). Muhammad claimed to have a new revelation from God, but Jesus stated that the scriptures from God testified about Him (John 5:39–40).

The Resurrection of Jesus

Founders of every other world religion have been buried, and their bodies remain in their graves. Only Jesus defeated death. In Acts 2, when Peter was speaking to a crowd who shared the common worldview of belief in God, the statement of Jesus's resurrection led to thousands of baptisms. When Paul makes the same claim in Acts 17, in the context of Athenian philosophy, it leads to sneering by many and belief by only a few (v. 32–34). Yet no matter the audience, the apostles continually pointed to the resurrection to show others the one true God.

In 1 Corinthians 15:3–6, Paul states that Jesus appeared not just to the apostles, but also to more than five hundred brothers at one time, most of whom were still living when Paul wrote those words. He pointed to witnesses who could confirm his message. This is important because it reminds us that the resurrection story was not a legend developed after the first century. It was a clear message taught by Christians from the beginning.

The Inspiration of Scripture

At the beginning of the first gospel sermon, Peter made it clear that the source of the miraculous tongue speaking was not drunkenness, but the power of God (v. 15). He immediately showed their message was a continued prophecy from the God who spoke through Joel and David. The apostles knew the message they were sharing was divine. Here is the way Paul puts it in 1 Thessalonians 2:13:

> For this reason we also constantly thank God that when you received the word of God which you heard from us, you accepted it not as the word of men, but for what it really is, the word of God, which also performs its work in you who believe.

Just as the apostles' message was distinctive, the nature of the Bible itself distinguishes it from any other writing. A library of 66 books written by different authors, in different languages, across different cultures, the Bible reveals one consistent message. Can you imagine gathering a group of musicians together who spoke different languages and asked them just to play a song, without providing any notes or guidance? They might make noise, but they certainly would not produce a symphony. Only a book inspired by God could communicate that singular message.

Not only can we know our world had a Creator, but the blessing of the gospel is also that we can know that Creator. There is One God and Father of all. Through the incarnation of Christ, the resurrection of Christ, and the inspiration of scripture, we can know the God we serve and how to serve Him.

DISCUSSION QUESTIONS

1. Consider what Paul said in Romans 1:20 about God's power and nature being seen through

    what has been made. What aspects of our world point to a Creator?

2. What are some competing "gods" in our culture today? In what ways might they distract us or tempt us to give them our devotion and commitment?

3. Have you seen someone who was willing to stand up for his or her faith in Jesus, even when it was difficult? What did that person's example teach you?

4. Think about the claims Jesus made in His ministry. How was His teaching distinctive from anyone else's?

5. If you were talking to someone who said they did not believe in the God of the Bible but were willing to study the subject, where would you begin? What principles from life or passages from scripture would be helpful?

ENDNOTES

1 N.T. Wright, and Michael F. Bird. *The New Testament in Its World.* (Grand Rapids: Zondervan Academic, 2019), 455.

2 Lawrence Mykytiuk. "Did Jesus Exist? Searching for Evidence Beyond the Bible," (*Biblical Archaeology Review* Jan/Feb 2015).

Only One God?

Andrew Phillips

When I was growing up, my little sister tried to make some extra money by selling me an item she had in her room. She was in elementary school, and she told me she would be willing to part with a valuable autographed baseball for the right price. She never explained how she came into possession of it, and I don't remember how much she was asking for it, but I can clearly picture her handing me the baseball and carefully watching my reaction. She had taken one of her markers and signed the ball in print with what was clearly her handwriting. Even more telling, she told me it was signed by Hank Aaron, but the name on the ball was spelled with only one "A." I was confident Hank Aaron would have known how to spell his own last name!

In that case, I did not have to see a copy of the genuine article to be able to spot a fake. But it is not always so easy. For example, law enforcement officers often have to reckon with the use of counterfeit currency. Kenda Creasy Dean explains that when FBI agents are learning to detect counterfeits, they do not spend much time studying the counterfeit bills themselves. They focus instead on the genuine article. That way, they can easily recognize what is real and what is counterfeit.[1]

In the same way, the more we study the nature of God as revealed in scripture, the more easily we will be able to spot descriptions of God that fall short of it. In Ephesians 4, Paul has already pointed out there is only one God. Once the exclusive nature of that claim is established, it is important to explore the unified nature of that claim – God is one.

GOD IS ONE.

Throughout the Old and New Testaments, scripture emphasizes the "oneness" of God. Deuteronomy 6:4 contains the "shema," which begins with the phrase, "Here, O Israel: The Lord our God the Lord is one." In Isaiah 45:5, we read, "I am the Lord, and there is no other, besides me there is no God." Paul reminds Christians in Corinth "there is no God but one" (1 Corinthians 8:4). In comparison to pagan cultures that worshipped many gods, the call for serving One God is clear throughout the Bible.

GOD IS THREE-IN-ONE.

And yet, scripture is also clear that the Father, Son, and Spirit are each distinct but also divine. For example, consider how each of these passages emphasizes divine nature:

> Matthew 5:45— "so that you may be sons of your Father who is in heaven. For he makes his sun rise on the evil and the good, and sends rain on the just and the unjust."
>
> Hebrews 1:3 — "He [the Son] is the radiance of the

glory of God and the exact imprint of his nature, and he upholds the universe by the word of his power."

1 Corinthians 2:10–11 — "these things God has revealed to us through the Spirit. For the Spirit searches everything, even the depths of God. For who knows a person's thoughts except the spirit of that person, which is in him? So also no one comprehends the thoughts of God except the Spirit of God."

The Father, Son, and Spirit are each described as the eternal God. Over the years, the terms "trinity" and "godhead" have been used to describe how God is three-in-one. The term "trinity" never appears in scripture, and "godhead" is a translation of Greek words regarding the divine nature, and it is used three times in the King James Bible. While the Bible does not explicitly use the word trinity, there are multiple examples of God working that illustrate the role of Father, Son, and Spirit.

For instance, we see the Father, Son, and Spirit present in creation. Genesis 1:1–2 tells us both that God created the heavens and the earth, and also that the Spirit of God was moving over all the surface of the water. The Father was acting in creation, along with the Spirit. John 1:1–3 states,

In the beginning was the Word, and the Word was with God, and the Word was God. He was in the beginning with God. All things were made through him, and without him was not any thing made that was made.

Since all things were made through Jesus, we know the Son was active in creation as well.

Another place we see each person of the Trinity present

is in the baptism of Jesus. Here is how Mark 1:10–11 describes it:

> And when he came up out of the water, immediately he saw the heavens being torn open and the Spirit descending on him like a dove. And a voice came from heaven, "You are my beloved Son; with you I am well pleased."

In this moment, we see God the Son incarnate, being immersed by John. The voice of the Father comes from Heaven, confirming the identity of Jesus as the Son of God, and the Spirit descends like a dove. The unity of the Godhead is on full display.

When Paul writes to Christians in Rome, he shares how the Father, Son, and Spirit are all at work when we pray. Romans 8:26–27 describes what happens when we pray to the Father: "For we do not know what to pray for as we ought, but the Spirit himself intercedes for us with groanings too deep for words." Several verses later, in verse 34, we are reminded, "Christ Jesus is the one who died, more than that, who was raised—who is at the right hand of God, who indeed is interceding for us." When Christians pray to God, the Spirit helps us communicate those things that are too deep for words, and our mediator, Jesus Christ, is at the right hand of the Father interceding for us.

One reason why this description of "One God" is important in Ephesians is that the book itself points to the work of each member of the Godhead. For example, Ephesians 1:11 discusses the purpose of the Father, 1:12 focuses on the hope in Christ, and 1:13 describes being sealed with the Spirit. Ephesians 2:18 states that in Christ, we have "access in One Spirit to the Father." Ephesians

3:16–17 reveal Paul's prayer that the Father would strengthen them with "power through his Spirit in your inner being, so that Christ may dwell in your hearts through faith." Even in worship, Paul encourages them to be "filled with the Spirit" (Ephesians 5:18) while "giving thanks always and for everything to God the Father in the name of our Lord Jesus Christ" (Ephesians 5:20). Throughout the book, Paul continually points to the unity in purpose of the Father, Son, and Spirit.

OTHER APPROACHES

There have been efforts to summarize the nature of the Godhead that fall short of the Biblical picture. It is important for us to be able to identify and resist those descriptions. One approach focuses on the Father, Son, and Spirit as three individual deities who work together as if they are players on the same team. This essentially amounts to a form of "polytheism," the worship of multiple gods.[2] This approach is inconsistent with the many scriptures that describe the "oneness" of God, and it essentially falls into the same temptation Israel often faced from surrounding pagan nations.

Another understanding envisions one god who created the other two. There are various versions of this line of thought, usually referred to as "subordinationism."[3] These thoughts prompted questions explored by church councils throughout the years. Was Jesus eternal or created by God? What about the Holy Spirit? The passages of scripture we have studied already show us the divine nature of Father, Son, and Spirit. A mindset of subordinationism does not hold up under scrutiny.

Another approach would describe one God revealing

Himself to us in various ways. We know what it is like for one person to possess several different roles. For example, I am a husband, a father, a son, and a brother all at the same time. This understanding would say there is only one being that relates to people in different ways, referred to as "modalism."[4] However, this does not fit with the distinct persons of the godhead we read about in scripture. For example, the Father, Son, and Spirit are all present at the same time in the baptism of Jesus.

None of the approaches listed above accurately captures the Biblical picture of God's nature. While it is a mystery, we hold to God's description of Himself: Three-in-One. One of the challenges in understanding the relationship of Father, Son, and Spirit is the limitation of our own language. Our human categories will never be broad enough or deep enough to completely comprehend the God we serve. We often try to think of physical analogies that encompass His nature, and though they are well-meaning and can push us to think in new ways, none of them can truly describe the Trinity.

Yet that should encourage us rather than discourage us. After all, the fact that we cannot understand God is a reminder of His divine nature. A God we could completely comprehend would be no more powerful than us. The fact that His ways are not our ways (Isaiah 55:8) is proof of His divine nature. That is why it is vital for us to continue to study and learn from the character of God and, of course, accept no counterfeits.

Discussion Questions

- What misconceptions about God's nature exist in our culture today? What can we do to lovingly teach the truth in those cases?
- Can you find other passages in the New Testament that emphasize the divine nature of Jesus?
- Can you find other passages in the New Testament that emphasize the divine nature of the Holy Spirit?
- As we review passages of scripture that show the Father, Son, and Spirit working together, are there any implications for how we as Christians should work together in the family of God?
- Why is it comforting to know we will never completely comprehend the nature of God?

Endnotes

[1] Kenda Creasy Dean. 2010. *Almost Christian: What the Faith of our American Teenagers is Telling the Church,* (Oxford: Oxford University Press, 2010), 89-90.

[2] Jack Cottrell. *The Faith Once For All Delivered,* (Joplin: College Press, 2002), 73.

[3] Ron Highfield. "Does the Doctrine of the Trinity Make a Difference?" in *Theology Matters: Answers for the Church Today,* ed. Gary Holloway, Randall J. Harris, and Mark C. Black. (Joplin: College Press, 1998), 22.

[4] Highfield, 23.

SCRIPTURE INDEX

CREDITS

van.com The "NIV" and "New International Version" are trademarks registered in the United States Patent and Trademark Office by Biblica, Inc.®

Scripture quotations marked HCSB are been taken from the Holman Christian Standard Bible®, Copyright © 1999, 2000, 2002, 2003 by Holman Bible Publishers. Used by permission. Holman Christian Standard Bible®, Holman CSB®, and HCSB® are federally registered trademarks of Holman Bible Publishers.

Scripture quotations from The Authorized (King James) Version. Rights in the Authorized Version in the United Kingdom are vested in the Crown. Reproduced by permission of the Crown's patentee, Cambridge University Press.

Scripture quotations are from the ESV® Bible (The Holy Bible, English Standard Version®), copyright © 2001 by Crossway, a publishing ministry of Good News Publishers. Used by permission. All rights reserved.

Scripture quotations taken from the (NASB®) New American Standard Bible®, Copyright © 1960, 1971, 1977, 1995 by The Lockman Foundation. Used by permission. All rights reserved. www.lockman.org.

Contributors

Jeremy Barrier (PhD Brite Divinity School, Texas Christian University) is Professor of Biblical Literature at Heritage Christian University, Florence, Alabama, USA.

W. Kirk Brothers (PhD Southern Baptist Theological Seminary) is President of Heritage Christian University, Florence, Alabama, USA.

Nathan Daily (PhD Claremont Graduate University) is Vice President of Academic Affairs and Professor of Religion at Heritage Christian University, Florence, Alabama, USA.

Ed Gallagher (PhD Hebrew Union College) is Professor of Christian Scripture at Heritage Christian University, Florence, Alabama, USA.

Justin Guin (MDiv Freed-Hardeman University) is Adjunct Instructor at Heritage Christian University, Florence, Alabama, USA. He has served the Double Springs Church of Christ (Double Springs, Alabama) as the youth/associate minister since 2004.

Michael D. Jackson (EdD Union University) is

President-elect of Heritage Christian University, Florence, Alabama, USA.

Andrew Phillips (PhD Regent University) is an Adjunct Instructor at Heritage Christian University, Florence, Alabama, USA. He has preached for the Graymere Church of Christ in Columbia, Tennessee, since 2011.

Future Berean Study Series Titles

Upcoming themes for the Berean Study Series are:

Someone Is Coming: Prophecies of Jesus (2027)

Someone Is Here: Teachings of Jesus (2028)

Someone Is Coming Again: Return of Jesus (2029)

Cypress Publications

Onesimus Bible Study Series

Confident of Your Obedience: Favorite Sermon on the Mount Texts (2025)

Refreshing the Saints: Favorite Old Testament Texts (2024)

Love of the Faith: Favorite New Testament Texts (2023)

Radiant Study Series

Invited: At the Table with Jesus (Fall 2026)

Outrageous: The Words of Jesus That Turn Our World Upside Down (2025)

Portraits of God's People (2024)

In Christ Alone: A Look at Blessings in Ephesians 1 (2023)

Jesus Loves Families Series

The Two Shall Become One Flesh: Studies for Christian Parents (2026)

What God Has Joined Together (2025)

To see full catalog of Heritage Christian University Press
and its imprint Cypress Publications, visit
www.hcu.edu/publications

9 798897 330195